PIMLICO

684

LONDON RECORDINGS

David Sylvester (1924–2001) was a critic of
international standing, an authority on contemporary art, and author of key works on
Magritte, Henry Moore and Francis Bacon, as
well as the acclaimed collections of essays *About
Modern Art, Interviews with American Artists,* and
the short account of his early life, *Memoirs of a
Pet Lamb.*

By the same author

Henry Moore

Interviews with Francis Bacon

René Magritte

Catalogue raisonné of René Magritte
(5 vols, editor and co-author)

Looking at Giacometti

About Modern Art: Critical Essays

Looking Back at Francis Bacon

Interviews with American Artists

Memoirs of a Pet Lamb

LONDON RECORDINGS

———

DAVID SYLVESTER

PIMLICO

Published by Pimlico 2005

2 4 6 8 10 9 7 5 3 1

Copyright © Estate of David Sylvester 2003

David Sylvester has asserted his right under the Copyright,
Designs and Patents Act 1988 to be identified as the author of this work

First published in Great Britain by Chatto & Windus 2003

Pimlico edition 2005

Pimlico
Random House, 20 Vauxhall Bridge Road,
London SW1V 2SA

Random House Australia (Pty) Limited
20 Alfred Street, Milsons Point, Sydney,
New South Wales 2061, Australia

Random House New Zealand Limited
18 Poland Road, Glenfield,
Auckland 10, New Zealand

Random House South Africa (Pty) Limited
Endulini, 5A Jubilee Road, Parktown 2193, South Africa

Random House UK Limited Reg. No. 954009

A CIP catalogue record for this book
is available from the British Library

ISBN 0-7126-1605-5

Papers used by Random House UK Limited are natural,
recyclable products made from wood grown in sustainable forests.
The manufacturing processes conform to the environmental
regulations of the country of origin

Printed and bound in Great Britain by Clays Ltd, St Ives PLC

For Lynne Cooke

CONTENTS

INTRODUCTION

'Quick,' hissed David Sylvester, 'get your shoes off! The guard won't be back for five minutes!' It was after hours in the Hayward Gallery, where he was showing me round perhaps the most sumptuous and personally satisfying of all the memorable exhibitions he curated: 'The Eastern Carpet in the Western World'. In no time we were over the protective rope and in the middle of this glorious object. Briefly, we silently padded around and had resumed our tour by the time the security man returned.

Presumably David had the authority to do what he liked, but to have walked legitimately across every carpet in the show would not have been nearly as memorable as that one illicit escapade. Carpets legendarily have magical associations. They are desert gardens, dream machines. That was the point he made by his fleeting action. It was also a game, and David loved games, intellectually and competitively; but more than that it was a true 'Open Sesame', which is what art is.

No critic or curator believed this more passionately than David or did more to make it happen. As Howard Hodgkin, interviewed here, recalls: 'One of the most important things is that he wasn't an intellectual but an artist, which made him very frightening as well as very frightened.' David recognised this. To John Mills, who first inspired him to collect carpets, he once exclaimed: 'Of course, I am not interested in ideas. I am interested in things!' His daughter Xanthe describes non-stop family sight-seeing tours centred on Venice and Rome when she was a teenager, David admonishing his children, 'Don't look at the guide book just look, just look!' and, in the presence of Bernini's *Ecstasy of Saint Theresa*, sighing an ecstatic 'Aaaaaaaaah!'

Although work took preference, his paternal pride was the match of any father's. His eldest daughter Catherine recalls that everyone remembers her first and only words for many months as a baby were 'Daddy' and 'doggie'. But David would have none of it. He had heard his blue-eyed girl's first word and it was 'rhododendron'.

David's solemn and sagacious persona was the expression of his commitment; a gravitas which could be intimidating. He slowed down conversation to his own disconcerting and hypnotic pace. So slow, he was not re-engaged as a radio critic because of what producers called 'the Sylvester pause'. A David pause could indeed be spectacular. On a drive to Brighton Tony Snowdon asked him a question in Reigate and only received a stentorian 'yes' as they came within sight of the Royal Pavilion. Such considered silences were the equivalent of the crucial spaces in his exhibitions; or the punctuation which, misplaced only once, would ruin a published article.

He was a perfectionist, therefore doomed to disappointment. '"Do you think it's any good? Do you think it's any good?" He always had those doubts the whole time,' explains his daughter Naomi. 'He was modest,' she continues, laughing as she adds, 'but I think some of it was put on.' His essay 'Curriculum Vitae', written in 1996, is nonetheless a pitiless and largely negative summing up, cast with the cold eye of age. The crumb of comfort is its conclusion, pronounced by Picasso: 'In the first place there isn't any solution, there never is a solution, and that's as it should be.' At least, in our shared frustration, we are not alone. And yet what fulfilment his summary reveals – as a critic of film and sport as well as art, a teacher, editor, committee man, curator, interviewer, broadcaster, film maker and general animator extraordinary. It pleased him when his radio producer, the film critic Philip French, praised him as a 'critic of the arts' rather than an art critic.

David lived to see a time of great doubt in the future, which has surely encouraged the quick artistic fixes and disdain for history now prevalent; but he blossomed as a critic in the period of post-war hope, and to the end took a long and optimistic view. His own art collection, which he refined and re-positioned as tirelessly as any exhibition, was almost entirely antique.

David's Orthodox childhood left him devoutly secular but there was no denying the rabbi in his character and appearance. It was in his heredity. He had a rabbinical ancestry and, as he has written, his father should have been a rabbi. David was rabbinical in his search for truth, his respect for the word, his patient questioning and patriarchal appearance: the beard, the domed forehead, the melancholy eye, the generous ears, the wonderful smile, the rich tonality of voice, the corpulence and buoyant lightness. 'I saw the most extraordinary man named SYLVESTER,' Evelyn Waugh reported to a friend in 1953, 'and cannot get him out of my dreams night or day. He was an art critic & looked like an American soldier of the most alarming kind.' It was a period when David anticipated 1970s fashion by adopting a US army combat jacket as casual wear.

Once met, never forgotten was indeed the case. His autobiographical essay, 'Memoirs of a Pet Lamb', is testimony to his captivating conversation. Whether face to face or in the form of a Socratic dialogue by telephone, no one was more compelling in their attention or gave such lavish compliments. The searchlight moved on, inevitably, but while it lasted it was dazzling. All he asked of critics was that they cared, and he was as attentive to the views of children as he was helpful to young writers and artists.

According to his wife Pamela, his most memorable quality was this intensity of focus. She recalls a day in the 1960s at Melrose Road, where David worked at the dining table overlooking the front garden. That afternoon, it had been arranged that he would let in the chimney sweep. Later, when Pamela asked if the sweep had called, David looked blank. She rang the sweep to ask what had happened, only to be told: 'Oh, I called, Madam, and I rang and rang but nobody was in – only that cripple in the window.'

To the painter Cecily Brown, his daughter with Shena Mackay, he stressed the need for long looking and the superiority of natural light. When David visited her first exhibition at the famous Gagosian Gallery in New York he immediately asked for the lights to be switched off. Visitors thought the gallery was closed until they slowly discerned his Buddha-like figure in the semi-darkness. 'One of the great privileges of being with David was seeing exhibitions outside gallery hours. To look at the Pollocks at the Tate show as the light waned was amazing, they really began to jump off the wall,' Cecily remembers.

'David's sense of colour was demonstrated in his choice of clothes,' writes Shena Mackay, '– the blues and greens of his shirts and ties, turquoise, rose, gamboge, yellow or ochre against the perfect Mediterranean blue. When I remarked, early in our acquaintance that blue doesn't go with brown, he cited Cezanne's use of them and proved that they can look marvellous together by wearing them.'

He also maintained that burgundy, however good, always tasted the same, whereas each glass of a decent claret tasted different. David was indubitably a claret, the years only improving his endlessly refined performances. Of people as of wine, age reveals the true stature. David died at his zenith though, in the light of the last shows he curated – the series of consummate Fancis Bacon memorial exhibitions – who knows what marvels lay in store. The aphorism with which he opened a climactic tribute to Picasso was decidedly not applicable to himself: 'An old woman is the ruin of a woman; an old man is a non-man.'

Indivisible from David's love of things was his fascination with artists. He admired them with the awe of someone who had tried and failed, and understood them with an equal empathy. As he wrote in *About Modern Art*, some of his best thinking 'went into private conversation with artists . . . and one of my great sadnesses in regard to this book and to everything else I have published is that it contains virtually no traces of all that talk'. This is a laughable statement, coming from the author of *Interviews with Francis Bacon* and one of the key chroniclers of his artistic time. That he valued interviews highly explains his anxiety to complete this last selection, on which he laboured until his death. 'I'm dying but I can't see people because I've got too much work to do,' was his telephone valediction to those on the outer circle of his friendship.

The result is an *ave atque vale*, combining old friends and new, some indeed long dead: Henry Moore, for whom in youth he was a secretary, until he had to stop because 'we spent too much time arguing about art': William Coldstream, his employer at the Slade; and the dancer and choreographer Leonid Massine, who the boy David saw performing at Covent Garden. Massine is one of four non 'art' choices which registers the liberating range of his interest. His inclusion strikes a musical note enforced by the last of all the interviews, with the composer Harrison Birtwistle. This eclecticism, in itself a reproof of the academic closed shop, is sealed by the interviews with Mike Brearley, the formerly captain of the England cricket team, and Ken Adam, best-known as production designer of the James Bond films. The Brearley interview is a reminder that not only was cricket David's favourite game, but he was a sports writer for *The Observer* for several years from the mid-1950s ('the most testing literary exercise I have undergone'); and his first and greatest ambition, abandoned at the age of ten, was to be a cricketer. David liked to equate art and sport. 'Name your first XI,' was a favourite request, be it of painters, sculptors, films, whatever.

Ken Adam was a friend from prep school days, so David was especially pleased to arrange the catalogue and exhibition of his work at the

Serpentine Gallery. In his film criticism David deliberately subverted the snobbish status quo, which dismissed Hollywood as lowbrow. He argued that the cult of the director was a distortion of the culture of the movies, which was to entertain. That these populist views were aired in the impeccably highbrow *Encounter* magazine was a piquant irony, and they attained dramatic fulfilment when he succeeded in conferring the status of fine art on Ken Adam's set designs. This aspect of his work illustrates how elitism should not be confused with snobbery and highlights his admirable lack of envy. As John Craxton who, with Lucian Freud, was David's first artistic guide, points out: 'David, like so many art critics, really wanted to be an artist, but he never had a chip about it. It is symptomatic that critics often identify with unsuccessful artists and are envious of successful ones. David was the opposite. He liked to be 'with it'. David and Peter Watson [publisher and co-founder with Cyril Connolly of *Horizon* and co-founder of the ICA] were often together going around the galleries and, when in Paris, meeting and being introduced to Peter's painter and sculptor friends. Peter's wide eclectic and professional knowledge made him a key figure in the formation of David's taste and method; and was a crucial influence in that earlier period.'

The remaining interviews are with artists – from Bridget Riley, on the crest of the wave of her first success in the 1960s, to Douglas Gordon in 2001, whose work combines David's equal passion for fine art and cinema. There are also three essays – on Adam, Malcolm Morley and Tony Cragg. As an interviewer David, characteristically, is not out to score points but to seek knowledge. In life he was sociable and amused by gossip but as an interviewer he is concerned with the art, not the artist's life. There is no probing here about parents, childhoods, sex or politics; yet character is revealed. His fascination with the artistic process puts artists' at their ease. He speaks their language, identifies with their quest.

This introduction can only hint at the treasures in store. I shall focus on five of the interviews, which span the 40 years covered. The first is with Henry Moore, who David perhaps knew better than any major British artist, with the obvious exception of Francis Bacon. It hinges on the crucial division in the work between carving and modelling. The nub lies in the admission that for Moore 'the essence of sculpture' is stone. He has an arresting simplicity of phrase: 'People get this idea that stone-carving is hard work. It's not. It's very pleasurable, soothing work . . . It's more like digging a garden.' And confirms that to see his sculpture at its best, in 'nature', one must travel to Glenkiln in Dumfriesshire.

The second is an interview in two parts, interestingly done at an interval of over a decade, with the painter William Coldstream. Coldstream was renowned for his wit and self-deprecating charm, typified by his comments on commissioned portraiture: '. . . if you have great difficulty making yourself work, like I do, when the sitter's really going to arrive, you've jolly well got to be there and ready and paint, whether you feel like it or not. It's much more easy to put a model off that you're paying than to put a sitter off who one hopes is going to pay one.' The 'one hopes' is quintessential Coldstream. Despite his reliance on precisely plotted measurement Coldstream regards art as a mystery, the inevitable reflection of our own: '. . . it's terribly difficult to really know a lot about oneself.' Although, typically, he shies from anything that might sound pompous: '. . . it probably isn't any higher form of activity than trying to solve crossword puzzles.' He concludes, '. . . I would tend to say off the cuff that all artists really paint for themselves'. That Coldstream taught for most of his career lends special weight to this observation.

Film buffs will surely delight in the essay and interview devoted to Ken Adam. David's opening sentence unarguably states the neglected right of the art director to be ranked in importance with any other film creator: 'there are moments in film when the set is more magnetic than the actors, the dialogue, the editing, the music.' This is certainly true of Adam: 'Is Bond Sean Connery? No, Bond is Ken Adam.' The more so as time went on and the films were no longer based on Ian Fleming's novels. David benefited from an insider's knowledge of film-making, having worked with Stanley Kubrick on *Lolita*; and he mentions that Spielberg, among many in the industry, rates Adam's war-room for Kubrick's *Dr Strangelove* as 'the greatest set in the history of cinema'. It was so convincing that even incoming American Presidents were surprised to find such a sanctum did not exist. Interviews have to be crafted as carefully as any other form of writing. The Adam interview has an especially deft and amusing punch-line.

'David felt at ease in the company of women, with men he felt a greater need to compete,' says Sarah Whitfield. When he interviewed Rachel Whiteread in 1999, he was old enough to be her grandfather. His customary respect is undiminished but there is a tenderness in the way he reveals this

– in my experience – shy artist to herself. 'DS: I would say your work was really a form of carving. RW: Yes. That had never occurred to me before.' One senses the shock of her surprise when he intuits her fascination with Egyptian art; and the sincerity of the compliment she pays when she divulges the secret ('I haven't said this to anybody before') that her *Book Corridors* was directly inspired by a certain old library in Hackney. There is flirtation: 'RW: Mmm. This could change my life, this conversation.' And engagement: 'RW: . . . Tony Smith do you like his work? DS: I like it very much.' It is an interview which deepens as it evolves. No wonder she rates it her best.

The Birtwistle interview is the last of the hundreds David conducted over a long lifetime, during which the tape-recorder had made the technique central to the artistic record. David is a master of the medium, so one instinctively takes particular note of his own promptings in this finale, conducted with great fortitude only days before he died. He can still laugh and his curiosity could be that of a man with a life time to look forward to. As with art and film, David had a practical experience of music, having tried to be a jazz saxophonist in his youth. It is unavoidable to sense the anguish of his own predicament in the question: 'Are you aware of how your music is heard? How it is listened to? And does it matter?' Perhaps the best interviews, in common with all art, are done by interviewers for themselves. We arrive once again at the mystery. 'I have a feeling . . . that painters often don't know what they're doing,' is the kernel of his last question. Like the shape of Bloom's journey through Dublin in *Ulysses* David arrives at a question mark – which, as Picasso said, 'is as it should be'.

Harrison Birtwistle adds a brief valedictory: 'David came back into my life after a long time, and for the last ten years we had what I felt was a sort of intellectual love affair – his death has made a great hole in my life, and in everybody's, even though they did not know him, and may not realise this.' *London Recordings*, along with all David's other books and writings, offers rich compensation.

John McEwen

HENRY MOORE 1963

Recorded June 1963 at Perry Green, Hertfordshire. Extracts from the version edited for broadcasting by the BBC were first published in the *Listener*, 29 August 1963. The present version has been edited from the transcript.

DAVID SYLVESTER *When you're working in materials like wood or stone, you're master of the result, but when you're working for casting in bronze you're not: somebody else intervenes. Does this irritate you?*

HENRY MOORE Well, it often does, because the casting problem today is a major headache for, I think, all sculptors – mainly because the number of sculptors has increased since the war by fifty-fold, I'm sure, and the bronze foundries haven't increased. So they're all doing much more work than they used to and they have to take on staff that's not trained. It is often a disappointment when a cast comes back from a foundry and it isn't as good as it should be.

What can go wrong with a cast?

Well, a cast can be not sharp enough because the wax original or the wax replica hasn't been cast clearly enough. That will then give you a cast that's dull all over, that's lost its sharpness. Then again, the cast may be too uneven in its thicknesses, so that in the cooling of the bronze a thick piece of bronze has to shrink more because there's more bronze to shrink than in a thin piece. Therefore you get distortions and you get twistings, perhaps.

How do you tell a good cast when one's delivered? I mean at first sight and apart from any obvious blurring.

Well, first one looks and it should be sharp. Then after that one knocks on it so that it rings. A good cast gives practically the same tone all over. You generally get better results when the sculpture is cast by the wax process rather than the sand process. The sand process tends to have a thicker top than the wax process does.

1

Is the advantage of a thinner cast simply that you're more likely to get an even thickness?

Well, one doesn't want it so thin that it could be damaged in transport or by knocks or bangs. But you want it as thin as it can be to keep its strength, so that in transport and in every other way you haven't an excess weight. If you have a head leaning forward and it's a solid head, that will have a bigger strain on a thin neck than if the whole thing is hollow. And this is why you can have a bronze standing figure perched on one foot, but you can't in stone. Because the bronze is empty above and therefore there isn't all this huge weight being just held up by one toe or something like that. But some Italian founders are so proud of doing a really thin cast that it's almost paper-thin and can be damaged in transport. Then there's the other kind which makes it so thick and so heavy that the weight increases the actual cost of the bronze, which is a very expensive material. A good founder will make it the right thickness for its strength, its full strength, but also be economical in the cost of bronze.

Where do you get most of your casting done?

I now have, because of doing rather larger things than I used to do, three or four different founders, because, if I only had one, I should be kept waiting two years for any new thing to be cast. So I have a foundry in Paris and one in West Berlin, and two or three in England.

What about the patination problem? Do you find that foundries can give you what you want?

No. I always patinate bronzes myself. I let them come from the foundry as a raw bronze, a natural bronze, which is rather like a dirty new penny, and then I'll decide whether the bronze is going out of doors in a clean atmosphere and therefore whether whatever patina I give it is likely to remain, or whether it's going into a chemical atmosphere, which may turn it black and therefore you might waste a lot of time in trying to make a certain patina that will be lost within six months. Also, one has conceived a sculpture from the beginning as a finished, complete bronze.

Sometimes I think of it as a dark bronze, sometimes I think of it even as a highly polished bronze. And all this only I can do. If I leave it to the bronze foundry, they certainly do it wrongly.

What do you have to do when the patina is going to include a variety of colour – say, with green and yellow and black and brown?

What one does sometimes is to prepare them for two or three days and then leave them out exposed, and the rain and the sun and the wind will give it a more natural sense. And then, if you think that a thing is beginning to look all right, then you can fix that by waxing it. And when it is waxed it will become a much more even and less varied and less colourful sculpture. But one tries with any patina to help the form of the sculpture rather than obscure it, just as the complexion in a person can help you to see what shape they are. If a young girl who is marvellous has a bad complexion, you don't notice how beautiful she may be. But if you get your complexion, as it were, fitting the form, then that's the ideal.

Obviously in using bronze you're able to do a good many things which you could never do in stone or wood. It gives all sorts of freedom and you can work bigger than it would be practical to work in stone. But do you sometimes get slightly irritated that bronze never really has the very satisfying surface which you get from stone? Does this frustrate you at all?

No. I've now learnt to like bronze very much indeed. No sculptor works direct in bronze: you can't. You can't take a block of bronze and cut it to the shape. You must make your object in something else, in plaster or clay, plasticine, anything. Wood even can be cast into bronze: those early Gothic gates at Hildesheim were carved in wood and then pushed into the sand in the ground, and the hole that they left was filled with bronze and this was their way of casting. So they're actual wood sculptures cast into bronze. Bronze is only a medium for making permanent a thing you've made in some other medium. It's a most wonderful and malleable material: it can do anything, almost. It's also almost indestructible. It lasts much much longer than stone, out of doors, anywhere you like.

It just doesn't have that marvellous luminosity of stone.

No. I still love stone. I'm much happier when I'm carving stone. But then I can get some of that pleasure in making my original, which gets cast into bronze, in plaster. Then you can build up, you can use an axe or a chisel, and you can mix the carving with the modelling technique. And that's why I like working direct in plaster. Because it's actually a mixture of carving as well as modelling. I still do some carving in stone or wood, but not as much; but working direct in plaster I still get a lot of the fun I used to get out of carving.

I take it that carving in stone especially is a much greater physical effort than carving in plaster.

No, no. A little bit, but not very much. No. The actual physical thing of carving is a matter of rhythm and of the muscles you use getting used to doing it. It's rather like walking. You work at a certain rate. But one can find stone-carvers of seventy still doing their full day's work of carving hard stones. People get this idea that stone-carving is hard work. It's not. It's very pleasurable, soothing work. It's perhaps in a way more pleasurable and more soothing than plaster because it takes longer. It's more like digging a garden.

Yes, but there's this funny thing about bronze in modern sculpture. I don't know whether it has to do with modern casting; I don't know whether it has to do with the relation between the kind of textures you get in modern art and the use of bronze; I don't know what it is. I mean, when you see a bronze by Donatello, or even when you see a bronze by Rodin, who's almost of our own time, the bronze seems perfectly right. Modern bronzes often seem – do you know what I mean? – a little bit uncomfortable. You don't feel that they've quite solved the problem. You know that the artist has had to use bronze because of its strength, because of its practicality, for many reasons. And yet you have a slight feeling of unease that the medium wasn't absolutely right for the idea, which is certainly not a feeling that you get with Donatello. Do you know what I mean?

Yes. Donatello's bronzes were all worked on by him afterwards. And this is what many people forget in looking at early bronzes. It's the same with the Greek bronzes and the Roman: practically all of them were worked

4

on by the artist, by the sculptor or his assistants after the casting. And this is what gives them the sense of their material, the sense of bronze, because they received their final shape in the material that they're completed in. And in that sense perhaps modern bronzes have lost something.

Do you think that modern artists work less on their bronzes?

Yes. Oh yes, I'm sure.

What about yourself? How much do you work on a cast?

For example, with the sculpture called *Knife-edge two-piece*, when it comes from the foundry it comes like a rough new penny. After that there are three weeks' work to prepare it before I begin the patination – work of filing and refining. For the knife-edge I've got on one of the pieces, the foundry couldn't possibly cut the cast to that sharpness. It has to be finished in the bronze. And this is what gives it, I think, its palette-knife thing. This is what one thought in having the idea of its being in bronze only. You couldn't make it in plaster; the plaster would break at that fineness. You couldn't make it in stone; it would break. That knife-edge thing is only possible in bronze. And, as I say, although it's a small work, twenty-eight inches long, there were three weeks at least of working on the bronze after it came from the foundry. Then there was another week or more of trying to get the patina so that the form showed and the bright bronze didn't give you only reflections of the room that it was in, and everything else. So that in some cases I work a long time on a bronze after it's cast.

You started casting in bronze rather than lead about 1937–8, didn't you? And the first big one was the Family Group *of 1948–9 with the passing of the baby from one parent to the other. And one gets the impression, you know, in looking at the early bronzes, that you were worried about the surface – that, for example, the smooth and characterless quality of the surface troubled you after using stone and wood. What was it that worried you, or still worries you, about the surface of the bronze?*

Now I'm beginning – and it's taken a long time – now I'm beginning to see the work, even in its maquette stage, as a bronze. I make the ideas for my sculpture always to begin with on a very small scale of only five or six inches, a size that I can hold in my hand and look at from on top, turn it in my hand and, by holding it close to my face, see it against the distance. And you can forget that it is a small thing: it can be any scale that you like. It's your mental scale, it's what you're thinking of it in the mind. And that's why I make my maquettes so very small. Once you make a thing a foot or two foot big, even if you intend later to make it much bigger, you have to get up and walk round it to see what it's like from all round. Whereas if you make it on a small scale, you're like the creator holding it in the palm of your hand. To begin with I used to find it difficult, because I hadn't had enough experience of what happened after making it in plaster for the bronze. And so one had to rethink again sometimes when it came back from the foundry. But now, as I make a thing even only two inches, three inches long, in my mind it is a life-size or over-life-size bronze. And with the twenty years that one has been doing so much bronze . . . This is why I think people like Rodin knew all the time what his sculpture was going to look like in the bronze. Now, a lot of the young sculptors of today, they've only had three, four, five years of knowing what's going to happen when it goes to the foundry and comes back.

Does this mean that nowadays, when you're working on your small maquette, you foresee, for example, which parts are going to be scored, which are going to be pitted, which are going to be more or less smooth, and so on? And therefore you think from the start of a certain shape in relation to the surface it's going to have.

No. No. The surface comes about from the way you do it. You can't possibly imitate the surface on a six-inch maquette.

I didn't mean imitate, but foresee it.

Yes, you foresee it a little bit, but you don't foresee entirely because the doing of a thing always changes it. And it depends on the size, too, that you use. This business of surface and texture should be, in my opinion, the outcome of how you do a thing and what degree of refinement of shape you want to get. If you want to get a knife-edge feeling, then that must be smoother than what it is if it's a great big rock, a solid thing; you can leave that rough. If you want to get the kind of tension between two muscles, you couldn't get that by a pitted surface, because there has to be a taut, stretched skin across it. Therefore it has to be more highly finished. So your texture should be the outcome of the refinement of shape which you want to get, and not the surface for its own sake.

When you talked before about the advantages of greater experience in the use of bronze, can you give an actual example of that?

Well, I wouldn't have had the experience before in handling plaster and working direct in it, or in the way I build even my armature for it: all those things. I now work much more direct. That is, I can do in a week what used to take me three weeks. When I'm working with plaster, I can foresee what it's going to look like much better than I used to do. And now, you see, what I do as well before a plaster goes to the bronze foundry is to colour it to imitate bronze, which is a very simple thing to do: you get bronze powder and shellac and you paint the sculpture very thinly, and it looks rather like bronze. At one time I used to send my plasters off as white plasters – like this one here. And as you see, with this large one in white, particularly out in the sunlight, that the underneath forms are getting reflection from the white plaster around them, so much so that the underneath forms are lit up, whereas in a dark bronze those will all be dark. Now all this changes, and I'm sure that I used to have big shocks when a thing came back from the bronze foundry. Now I don't because I make it look like a bronze before it goes.

And if there's something you don't like, you can start . . .

I change it. It's very simple. After the thing looks like a bronze it's very simple to add plaster or to take it off and to redo a thing.

When you're working in stone you can see the final colour all the time because you're working in the final material. When you're working in plaster for casting in bronze, given that plaster has this very peculiar white luminous quality, do you find it irritating that the surface you're seeing is so very different in colour from the final material? Do you wish there were a kind of brown plaster or green plaster?

No. Because I think that white plaster, because it doesn't show the form as clearly as a dark material does, makes you in the beginning make your forms bigger and have a bigger relationship, because the little subtleties don't show up so well. And therefore you concentrate on the big things, and it's only towards the end that one colours it with a colour wash and then you see what the minor forms are doing. But to begin with the white plaster makes you make your big forms more telling than they would be, and not get interested in textures before the form's there.

This is something that has happened with some contemporary sculptors. Do you ever finish a thing in white plaster and really wish that this could be its final appearance and regret having to turn it into bronze for the sake of permanence? Does this sometimes happen with you, that you'd like it to be white?

Yes, yes, sometimes plaster will have a quality that you know will be lost when it goes into the bronze. But you can keep that one original plaster.

Have you ever thought of painting a bronze white? One or two people have, but you've never done that.

That seems to me a wrong way round.

You were telling me a little while ago that you didn't work in the old way any more, of beginning by drawing, filling sketchbooks with drawings, a variety of drawings, and go through these selecting things that seemed interesting ideas. Then you'd make a maquette from a drawing and go on from there. This was your technique for many years, wasn't it?

Yes. Being young, one had lots of influences mixed up in one's mind, so that this sorting out seemed sensible.

But you did it for a very long time.

I did it for a long time.

What you called 'drawing as a means of generating ideas'.

Yes. And also a means of sorting out the ideas, too.

And you did this from the beginning of your career?

Yes.

And you've only lately stopped?

Well, now what I find is that, when what seems to me a good idea comes, I recognise it a bit quicker than perhaps I used to do. I recognise them as good enough to sustain over a longer period.

May I get this idea straight about drawing as a means of generating ideas? I mean, how much automatism was there? In other words, in how many cases was it, as it were, when the pencil was on the paper that things were beginning to happen? Or were you actually carrying out things on paper which you had visualised clearly before you drew them?

Well, one used to use both methods. Sometimes you'd sit down with no idea at all, and at some point in the doodling, scribbling – whatever you call it – you'd see something in it. And from then on you could evolve the idea. And that would be a way of working, say, late in the evening, when one had a free mind. Early in the morning I used to find one would start off with a definite goal, a definite idea – that I could see a seated figure I'd want to do. And that in itself would lead to a lot of variations of the seated figure. That is, you'd give yourself a theme and then let the variations come, and choose from those which one seemed the best.

When you say you started with the idea that you wanted to do a seated figure, was that a verbal idea or did you actually have the seated figure visualised in your head?

9

You can begin from two opposite ways. You can begin with searching for a good sculptural idea or you begin with the human idea – say, the mother and child – and you try to make it become a good sculpture. That is, you amalgamate life and art, and how you do it, whether you start from the art side or the life side, in a way doesn't matter, as long as the amalgamation comes. I used to try to avoid visualising the finished product until a later stage. I mean, I remember writing little notes in one's sketchbooks saying such things as 'Don't do any more' – whatever it may be that one had done. These mental evaluations of what sculpture you want it to be would be in the back of one's mind, besides the ideas.

And you tried not to visualise?

Yes. Yes.

So, really, in the morning drawing as well as the evening drawing you were using drawing as a means of generating ideas.

Yes. Now, I still like drawing just as much as ever, but there seems to be less time to do the lesser activity. And so I'd be much more pleased to do at the end of a year three good pieces of sculpture than produce fifty good drawings. Sculpture is one's aim still and the shorter the time gets, the more it becomes one's aim.

Your main work in the last four or five years has been a series of multiple-piece reclining figures. Has any of those started from a drawing?

No.

And what was the last important work you did that did start from a drawing?

I think the *Family Group* ones probably. The family group ideas were all generated by drawings. And that was perhaps because the whole family group idea was so close to one as a person. We were just going to have our first child, Mary, and it was an obsession. One could have turned out three hundred drawings a day if one had liked on this theme.

1963

The warrior figures, which started in 1952, didn't begin from drawings?

The warriors began from a little pebble that led one on from a stump of a leg to add to it the back and to add to it the arm and the shield. This you couldn't do by drawing.

I wasn't aware at the time of the fact that you'd given up working from drawings, but I did feel that your sculpture was becoming more concerned with tactile experience and with motor experience rather than visual experience. And it's interesting that the time when I, as a spectator, felt this was going on in the finished work was the time when you were not beginning with a drawing any more, but were beginning with a kind of experience which couldn't be expressed in drawing. But you said that the first warrior began from a found object. Did a lot of the recent sculptures begin from found objects?

Finding driftwood and pebbles and bones, anything that starts one off with a reality which one alters and changes, for me now is a much better start than a drawing.

Do you take these actual objects and add plaster or clay to build up an idea?

No. What I do is, I look at them, handle them, see them from all round, and I may press them into clay and pour plaster into that clay and get a start as a bit of plaster, which is a reproduction of the found object. And then add to it, change it. In that sort of way something turns out in the end that you could never have thought of the day before. This to me now is the beauty of each day if one's working – that by the end of it you might have had something happen that you couldn't possibly have foreseen. And this is why, if one misses a day of work, sometimes I think, well, that day might have produced a much better idea than I've had in any of the months that's gone before. And just because one missed that day, perhaps one missed the very idea that might have been the best of the year.

Have any of the two-piece and three-piece reclining figures begun from found objects?

Yes, some of them have. That extra piece of ground that we've got down below there – I think that down there must have lived a butcher who did the preparing of his carcasses and everything else, because all over, whenever the garden is dug, we find bits of old bones sawn across. And these always can start me off with an idea. But of course the idea must be in your mind to begin with; whatever you see in nature is already in your head. You can't think of an idea that's not already prepared for.

This is shown by the fact that people find flints and shells on the beaches and in fields which they put on their mantelpieces because they remind them of sculptures by yourself.

Well, this may be the value of certain kinds of modern sculpture, that it opens people's eyes to nature and they pick up things which they wouldn't look at otherwise. And it just means that they look at things with a new eye.

This is one of the ways in which the twentieth century has made nature imitate art. I mean not just in the larger view of seeing a landscape as Claude saw it, but in seeing something as small as a pebble the way an artist has seen it. But you've always collected these pebbles and bones, you've collected them for more than thirty years. Did you previously use them as beginnings for a sculpture?

Not as much as I may do now. You see, to begin with I was a stone-carver; for me stone was the essence of sculpture. It still is, really. But the sort of effort that was needed to take a hard lump of stone and turn it into a willed work was what sculpture was. And I still have that admiration for stone sculpture.

When you did stone sculpture in the Thirties, you couldn't incorporate found objects, but did you ever imitate them?

No. No.

You used their influence, but you didn't imitate them?

In those days one had to buy odd random pieces of stone from any stonemason that you found – pieces one could afford to buy. And they would be odd shapes. They wouldn't be sawn blocks in a geometrical square; they'd just be random blocks, so-called. And you'd then try to think: what piece of sculpture of the biggest size can I get into that? How can I make that into something in which I waste as little stone as possible? And sometimes a wonderful piece of stone would stay in the corner of one's studio for a year, two years, three years, because ideas you had would waste too much of that piece of stone in doing it. And I would worry how much stone was wasted. Perhaps that's a bad thing; perhaps it's not. But this was a very good discipline.

In the series of multiple-piece reclining figures, in which particular ones did you use found objects?

Well, for example, in the first of the three-piece sculptures which is going to be shown soon, one of the pieces, the middle piece, was suggested by a vertebra – of I don't know what animal it was – that I found in the garden. And the connection of one piece through to the other is the kind of connection that a backbone will have with one section through to the next section. But they've been separated. It's as though you've left the slipped disc out of them, but it's there. That's the only one I can immediately think of.

In short, nowadays, with your ideas for sculptures, the first form they take isn't a drawing in a sketchbook, but a sketch-model which may or may not incorporate some found object?

Yes.

And you do it five inches long or something?

Yes. As I was saying, I prefer to do a sketch-model a hand-size that one can turn round and control, as though you're God, as it were, as though you're the person holding it in the palm of your hand, and in this way you can create it without its being of any particular size whatever.

You mean, once you can hold it in the palm of your hand it has no scale at all?

It has a mental scale. I was looking the other night at a reproduction of a sketchbook of Leonardo's, and the book was filled with ideas for equestrian statues, about twenty to the page, with each little drawing no more than an inch high, but when you look at that you don't think of an inch, you think they're over-life-size. And this is what one can do in a sort of mental scale which really counts, and if you have a mental scale a thing can be fifty feet high or five feet high and it's still this monumental object; and this to me is the explanation of someone who has this monumental vision, and it's not to do with how big they do their paintings, it's something that's purely in their heads.

Working on the sketch-models, do they come fairly quickly to the realisation of an idea, or do you in fact work on them for a long time very often?

No. An idea comes quickly. You put it on one side and then in the studio something you did a fortnight previously catches your eye and you know straight away what is wrong with it and you make that alteration, and out of it then comes something that you are satisfied with or not.

At what point do the major changes tend to take place? Between the original form of the sketch-model and its final form at the time you discard it, or between the beginning of the larger projection of it and the final larger work? Where do the biggest changes happen?

The biggest changes are tried on the scale of the big work. You may think that you've been able to imagine something ten feet high, but when you look at something ten feet high and you are close to it, the angle that you look at is something that you can't imagine as a small thing.

No matter how experienced you are?

No matter how experienced.

A work of yours which would have been really rather big up till even as late as 1950 would now be quite a small work: your big works have got bigger.

1963

Obviously in certain cases, when you've been working in relation to certain buildings, this has been something demanded of you by the scale of the building, but apart from that you have had a tendency to make the bigger works bigger. Are you aware of what has driven you in this direction?

Well, to begin with I remember first making a Hornton stone reclining figure in Parkhill Road, Hampstead, which had three iron steps and then a turn and then another three iron steps to get into it, and carrying in a hundredweight bag of plaster was a problem. Therefore the stone sculpture that I did there, this reclining figure which was – what? – three feet long, was to me a major work, because getting it in and out every time I sent it to an exhibition cost me – whatever it was – seven pounds ten to get lorries to collect it and take it away. All this kind of thing: you're restricted by it. You may not think of it, but in the background are these problems. Whereas now, thank goodness . . . In fact, I'm urged by the architects of the Lincoln Center to make the sculpture I'm doing there bigger than I want to do it. It's practical reasons that now make it practical to do sculpture on this scale.

So your new studio down at the other end of the garden is much bigger than the studio you've used here for years?

If you work in the studio you never get more than three feet away from the sculpture that you're making. If that sculpture goes out of doors, you're going to have an awful shock, because you're going to see it for the first time from fifty yards away or a hundred yards. So if a sculpture is going out of doors it should be made out of doors. An outdoor piece of sculpture is often approached, perhaps, from nearly a hundred yards away. What you get out of it from fifty or a hundred yards away is very important; that's your first reaction. Also, with a piece of sculpture you're going to see it on a bad day, on a dull, miserable, foggy, wet day, or you're going to see it in brilliant sunshine – all these things have impact, and one should make a piece of sculpture that can stand up to all these different conditions, and it can only do that if it's like a really good person who is all right at a cocktail party, calm and peaceful and obtrusive and everything else. So that if you make a structure in the open air, especially in the English climate where you have these terrific changes, all these things have to be taken into consideration and I think you can't take in all those factors without experience in reality.

A great deal that has been written about your work has emphasised its landscape metaphors. But where are the landscapes that get into your work? You've been living here in Hertfordshire for twenty years or more, but you were brought up in Yorkshire. Are you aware of particular landscapes as shaping your work, influencing its forms? Are they always childhood landscapes; are they ever the landscapes of Hertfordshire?

To me the slag heaps of Castleford and around Castleford in my youth were huge mountains; they were like the Alps. And when I go back and see them now, I see them in the same way. These heaps of slags, they have the same scale as the Pyramids. Now, the first rock, or natural piece of stone, I saw was a piece standing outside Leeds, at a place called Adel, and I went there as a boy of about twelve or thirteen. I'm sure if I went back it would only be the size of this room, but to me it had a mountainous impact.

And is there also anything of Hertfordshire in your work?

Hertfordshire is only a setting for things. There are no roughnesses, there are no harsh impacts in Hertfordshire. The ideal setting for my sculpture is where those four things of mine are which Tony Keswick has in Scotland, near Dumfries, in a landscape which is, I should say, exactly as it was thirty million years ago, untouched by man. It's not a suburban garden, it's not a cultivated parkland, it's nature, it's landscape as primitive man saw it.

And that part of Scotland, does it resemble your part of Yorkshire?

A little bit. There are parts of Yorkshire that are like that.

The parts that you knew?

I think sometimes it's not the parts that one knows so much as the parts that you're taken to and which open up a whole outlook that you hadn't realised.

16

It looks to me as if certain landscapes you didn't see as a child influenced the second Two-piece Reclining Figure. *The bottom half of that figure is very much a rock. The first thought that I had when I saw it was that you had been influenced by Monet paintings of Belle-Île and Etretat. And then about a year after first seeing this sculpture I came across a picture postcard that you'd sent me when you'd been on holiday the summer before you did this figure. It showed the rocks off the shore at Bournemouth that are called the Old Harry Rocks, and I thought they were exactly like the lower half of this figure. I don't know whether you remembered these rocks consciously when you were doing the figure, but the resemblance amazed me.*

No. I think sometimes the obvious influences in your work you shut out. I don't know why, but perhaps one doesn't want to admit influences.

How did you come to the idea of the three-piece reclining figures as against the two-piece ones?

The two-piece sculptures pose a problem like the kind of relationship between two people. And it's very different once you divide a thing into three. Then you have two ends and a middle. In the two-piece you have just the head end and the body end or the head end and the leg end, but, once you get the three-piece, you have the middle and the two ends, and this became something that I wanted to do, having done the two-piece. I tried several little ideas before this one and what led me to this solution was finding a little piece of bone that was the middle of a vertebra, and I realised then that perhaps the connection through of one piece to another could have gone on and made a four- or five-piece, like a snake with its vertebrae, right through from one end to the other. But three is enough to make the difference from two. That is what one tried to make: it's a connecting-piece, carrying through from one end to the other like you might have with a snake. In a way, the more pieces you make, the easier it is. If you made a figure of ten pieces, then this dividing up would become a formula. The problem probably is more difficult when you're dividing into two only than if you divide it into three. Certainly it would be easier in four or five, so that there comes a certain stage where the problem has its maximum exhilaration for you to solve, and I think probably a three-piece is as much as one would want to attempt.

LEONIDE MASSINE 1974

Recorded 16 May 1974.

DAVID SYLVESTER *I imagine there was a big difference between working with artists like Bakst and Goncharova, who were essentially stage designers, and on the other hand with artists like Picasso and Matisse and Derain and Miró and Masson, who came in from outside and were involving themselves in the theatre for the first time.*

LEONIDE MASSINE Easel painters, yes, easel painters. The answer, I think, lies in that; that the so-called scenic artists are at certain moments very limited, whereas real artists such as have existed in history, they have no limits. Their art is not measured by any particular measure. Scenic artists have limits and I dare say I think I was a little bit instrumental in that because when I saw Picasso, when I saw Matisse, I realised that it is nonsense to remain in scenic art, you understand. Of course it was Diaghilev who made me know Picasso and Derain and Matisse. Through him they all came to ballet, but to me there was no question how much more valuable their work was for the creation of new ideas.

And they all seemed to be able to adapt themselves quite quickly to the needs of the theatre?

Oh, there was that very extraordinary thing: they bent a little bit and we bent a little bit and our arms joined.

And it usually worked?

You have just mentioned one of the first: after my quarrel with Bakst, it was André Derain, easel painter; then came *Tricorne*. The answer is right in the realisation; then came Matisse, *Le Rossignol*; not one mistake. As he put it, there it was.

And Jeux d'Enfants, *with Miró.*

19

Jeux d'Enfants also, then even Dalí. In that particular case I was so fascinated by what he was doing that I let him lead; he was really the main figure when I worked with him because his ideas were extraordinary; it was not even a case of suggesting something of my own. I followed strictly what he suggested.

Were there other people with whom you felt you had to take that part of playing second fiddle?

Generally yes, generally yes; Matisse the same thing.

Matisse the same thing?

Yes, yes.

You're very modest in your attitude, aren't you?

Well, you see this is not really modesty. I think this is a very logical way to work with an artist because after all there's a great difference between a youngster who starts his career in the ballet – a very limited world – and such giants like Matisse, like Picasso. Here is the answer; and Dalí's amongst them in his own way.

So you are really saying that ballet is no more dance than it is design and music, and so on, and that it is not a matter of the other elements being subordinate to dance?

Diaghilev very justly said that the spectacle of ballet consists first of all of course of the author, of the poet or writer, of the composer, of the painter and the choreographer; it's *one* of the four elements.

One of the four elements.

Nothing more and he's dead right, I think, on this. It's no use to try to beat everyone because you're just taking away from your vital collaborators; you live by them, they bring you up. If you have a good author, a good painter, a good composer, what is more extraordinary is that then you too are lifted.

But of course this would be a radically different position from Petipa's, wouldn't it, for whom I take it dance was primary?

Yes, in his opinion it was like that; but let us see what are the results. What would be *Swan Lake* without Tchaikovsky's remarkable score? What would be the *Sleeping Beauty* without Tchaikovsky's remarkable score? At that time Ivan Vsavolojsky was director of the Imperial Theatre, and he was an intelligent and cultured man, enough to suggest already that ballet is not just ladies on points, turning on points, in pink tutus, you see.

In your autobiography you talk again and again of the way that a particular kind of painting has inspired you, of how ideas for a certain kind of movement or a certain ballet have been inspired by some painting that you've seen. Did you talk to your collaborators about this?

No, this was directly for me; if I see a Simone Martini, it is me who was shocked by it, you see; if I see Tintoretto, his colour, in the Scuola of San Rocco, it is me who was impressed directly. I think they work directly on my imagination at first sight.

But, I mean, how much did you talk to the designers about these ideas?

Oh, I might mention that in discussion.

Have you ever felt a desire almost to design the costumes yourself or to design the sets yourself?

No, I followed the principle – how could I touch something else if I don't know my own craft? Why should I put my hand to literature and poetry when I'm only at the very beginning in my own craft, with so much to discover? That's the first thing. And secondly, I believed firmly that such a mixture would lead to dilettantism of a very mediocre kind, and I found it was always so – everybody tried, but they never succeeded.

Did you feel at the time, and do you feel now, that the kind of different elements in Parade *worked successfully together – the purely Cubist element*

*of the Managers' costumes and the design of the performers' costumes – did
you feel that this worked as an aesthetic whole?*

I feel it was the most interesting experience of that period and the fact is
that for some reason everybody tried to understand this work. Why is
that? I always say, well, it hadn't got the importance of *Sacre du
printemps*, but there were some elements which were very, very avant-
garde and which gave the incentive to go away and search. And certainly
the Picasso point of view on these various old-measure characters gave
the character to the whole thing. I think it was a really worthwhile thing
to remember now.

It was curious because, before you started to choreograph Parade, *they'd
already gone quite far with the planning of it, hadn't they?*

Yes, Cocteau.

And Picasso had been working on it too.

To a certain extent, but you see there was again Diaghilev who exerted a
certain discipline on Cocteau. You know at a certain moment there was
an argument about voices coming through megaphones and Diaghilev
said no, it can't be done because we are in choreography, so express it by
that means, not by others.

Yes, he was right, wasn't he?

Certainly.

*Did all the easel painters who worked with you and who worked with
Diaghilev stay around for such a long time, in the course of rehearsal and the
creation of a ballet, as Picasso did?*

No, perhaps not, but the reason for that was that Picasso was attracted by
Olga Kokhlova to such an extent that when we did *Les Femmes de bonne
humeur*, which was a Bakst production, Picasso painted the props.

But with Tricorne *too: he stayed in London for three months.*

Oh yes, yes. Well, at that time he was very flexible and he had understood the importance of contributing something to the spectacle which Diaghilev conceived in that way: the best of painting, the best of music, the best of everything.

I remember the first time I saw Tricorne. *The thing that struck me very forcibly was in the dance at the end, with all the people on the stage – the dance based on the* Jota. *I thought it was one of the most miraculous combinations of movement and design that I've ever seen. The way in which the movement and the colour worked together to make a kind of moving kaleidoscope, and the way in which the dancers were constantly re-forming, the groups constantly re-forming, and each time they re-formed there was another marvellous balance of colour, which gave a kind of ideal of collaboration between design and movement. When you created this ballet were the costumes actually being worn during rehearsal?*

No.

They weren't?

No.

Picasso was watching the rehearsals presumably, of course?

You know he liked rehearsals much more than performances. He said I can see much more in the rehearsal.

Right. And you were seeing his designs evolve, you were seeing the costumes being made?

Yes.

I mean, was it just some marvellous kind of chance that each time that the group of dancers re-forms there's another extraordinary configuration? Did you have it in your mind in designing the movements and the configurations of the dancers? To what extent were you thinking about the colours Picasso was using?

It came without much deliberation. I believe the answer to this is that very justly Picasso took a certain volume for the peasants, for peasants of Seville, and he completed it by welding the whole of Spain into one thing; instead of going to one province or another, he brought them all together.

Again it probably came from Diaghilev and as they have this extraordinary character for *Jota Valenciana* in long skirts, mining men from the north around Bilbao, and all that mixed obviously with *matador* and *picador* to get the whole thing. So anywhere you put them it will always be good, you understand, because the characters are so well chosen. For Castallanas, for Sevillanas, he gave more volume and of his blue and green so marvellously chosen, so you could not make a mistake, impossible. He divided them in small pieces and there would be a *matador*, here would be a *picador*, here *Jota Valenciana*, here the man from the north – that's how it's worked out, it's by the unmistakable choice of the primary elements. Rhythm also, of course, is directly important to choreography as to the pictorial effect, so naturally if he does eight Sevillanas I will not break them into eight individuals; they all *do* the same thing. So it all came naturally together, but created by one man, Diaghilev; remember that.

Which of your works do you like best in retrospect?

Well, I think what stands out in my opinion would be *Sacre du printemps*, which I reworked; *Tricorne* I think; and perhaps *St Francis*.

It's very interesting that you don't mention the four symphonic ballets of the Thirties.

Yes, well, I don't mention them because there was the sort of desire of a young man who is in a square box and he's feeling that his imagination reaches much more forward and he's looking to come out of that impasse; that was the main thing. But let's quickly say that you can't accept that as a mature interpretation of a symphonic form; there is just a glimpse of it here and there.

1974

I am trying to think if there's a common element to the ones you pick out –
Tricorne *and the* St Francis. *It's* Sacre du printemps. *It's interesting that
you choose that since originally it was created by Nijinsky . . .*

Nijinsky's *Sacre*, although I haven't seen it, I admire very much.

You never saw it?

I saw only photographs and I saw a glimpse of dancers who had danced it,
who showed me some movements. It was a very, very revolutionary work,
let us say. After all the very gentle approach of Fokine in his works; and it
would take somebody of genius to do that. As the French say, '*C'est Gauguin
du printemps.*' It was ahead of its time. If he hadn't been so attracted and
hadn't had a fixed idea connected with Dalcroze's interpretation of music;
texturally the thing would live. But it was unbearable to hear and to see.

There was too much going on?

Yes, Diaghilev explained that scientifically: the law of the ear doesn't
correspond to the law of seeing. You can do it one by one, but when
joined together it is too much. The whole score was extremely
revolutionary as real music, and the fact was that Nijinsky had the very
right and interesting approach as choreographer, but he couldn't master
the relationship of counterpoint. So when Diaghilev asked me to do that,
I suggested meeting Stravinsky and I said: look, it's not possible to make
once again the same mistake – we've got to find an overall counterpoint
covering certain phases of your music, and he agreed before I started and
then the thing was more acceptable.

   Now I am about to compose to the piano concerto of Brahms, I have
taken as a dramatic theme that of '*Hymne à la beauté*' by Baudelaire,
which is a marvellous poem. Of course it is a try-out, you see. I don't
make a ballet out of it – it is treated in a rather peculiar form. My artists
do not come on stage because I thought that was a disturbing element.
It's an experiment, but I think I can succeed in it.

*And do you equate the piano with one group of dancers – or with a sole
dancer constantly throughout the thing – and the orchestra with another, or*

*is there no special link between them? Because you haven't done anything
before to a concerto, have you?*

No, but you see the sort of relief of certain passages is quite evident in it if
you remember the Baudelaire poem; it's quite extraordinary in strength
and expression. One line of his poem gives ideas for the whole
movement, but the '*La Beauté sortie de l'abîme*' or the '*Centre du ciel*'
describes it marvellously – that and all these elements are assembled as a
part that I have to fit to the mood of his concerto.

*At what point did you suddenly see the connection between the Brahms and
the Baudelaire? How did it click, this sudden vision of the connection?*

Well, it is like in much research work – you can't discover the whole
thing, but suddenly, by listening and by reading, at certain points things
do that; you see that they can make contact. And from that little spark in
one spot comes all the rest. You think if this exists in one point it must
exist in the others, and little by little it's justified. It's a very interesting
process – a process which leads to most fascinating things for me who
started to deviate from ballet a long time ago – to find new possibilities,
and I'm developing it now more and more.

And who is going to design it?

I don't know yet. I am only in the process of trying, like a layman, to put
stone like that, stone like that, stone like that, and finally see that that's
how it should be. I'm working with elements, you see, at present.

Your first interest in painting was in the Italian primitives?

I started with Byzantine art and that was the cornerstone of my
education; Italian history.

Were you drawn to that because of having been brought up with Russian icons?

No, not really. Well, that is quite true – I am Orthodox and we've had
many icons in our house. I have one even now, brought to me by my

father to Italy. But no, it was simply perhaps to see these remarkable things – mosaics and Byzantine things – in Rome, in Santa Maria Maggiore, or in Florence; mosaics that struck me as unbelievably beautiful, and at the same time they supported the mystic thought of religion without any possible criticism of it.

But when you first saw Cubist painting were you sympathetic to it? Did you already know when you were in Moscow the work of the Russian avant-garde?

No, I had little training in painting, but I was struck by Picasso, to such an extent that in *Sacre du printemps* I completely abolished lines. I was struck with his forms, with his Cubist forms in perspective, and that gave me *Sacre du printemps* right away, and so many years later now in Florence when I revived it, I was amazed to see how at the very beginning of my experience as a choreographer I had that desire to get away from the conventional lines and established symmetry of ballet, and that I intend to use very much. It was certainly a very, very vital thing to the future of choreography.

Cubism?

Oh yes. It permitted me to manipulate my groups in an entirely different way and to treat them as a volume, an organic volume of harmony, of counterpoint, of optical counterpoint, and a lot of devices which come from it, you see.

And at what point did you become conscious of doing this? When you first did Sacre *for Diaghilev?*

Yes, it was 1920.

And that influenced your later work too?

Well, unfortunately there was no more possibility, because that corresponded to that extraordinary score of Stravinsky's. Now I am coming back to it because I am more and more versed in the symphonic form. I believe this is a great reform and my book, which I am publishing soon in London,* tells the whole thing, not in words but in demonstrations. The great reform consists in a very brief statement: it's the first time in the history of all ballet that I have come to the conclusion that the movements have their harmony directly, precisely the same as in music. And that harmony is the main object of all creative work. Without it things are dead; be it in one form or in the other, it must exist. In music you can't listen to the music which has no harmonic context in chords, in the interpretation of the canto; it is the same thing in ballet, you can't look at the dry straight figures and say this is contemporary, that's nonsense. Harmony is of all time, it's an eternal thing, as old as man. As soon as man has come to the world he starts to move, and that's what I am about to do in the theory which I am developing.

I heard you say at rehearsal to a dancer whom you were criticising that a given posture was like a chord.

Exactly. It is a chord, it is a chord, and by this I establish the relationship of the few parts, the instruments, so to say, that the body possesses. They are not as many as they are in an orchestra, in music, but they are sufficient to elaborate the most interesting compositions. At the same time, of course, it is a must that a counterpoint of parts of the body must exist at all times and that all movements must be treated in three dimensions; they must be three-dimensional, and if we eliminate one of them for some reason, that reason must be strong enough. As we say this is a *Bas Relief* or this is an *Haut Relief*. Let's accept that all motion is in three dimensions: I soon know, in analysing work, I soon find my mistakes now; I don't need to go to the critics; I soon see what's lacking in the work in respect of rhythm, in respect of life of three dimensions, each one being there at all times. If we don't realise what we're doing, the audience will, they will see suddenly a body paralysed, they will see suddenly an arm that will repeat the same movement, and of course one of the primary things is putting the symmetry into its place. Because we have a right and left side, that doesn't mean that we have a right and left side in choreography, you see it's exactly the opposite. There are all sorts

* Leonide Massine, *Massine on Choreography, Theory and Exercises in Composition* (1976).

28

of symmetries acceptable to a very minimum extent. Symmetry is necessary because without it there will be an element missing. But I don't mean millions of productions all danced symmetrically; that's killing, that's a terrible poverty and misunderstanding of what the human being is and how it can be used. It still will be right for this historic, remarkable invention of classical dancing; it will be dead right there, but nowhere else. It is a closed form. So the new element of irregularity is what in fact we are now elaborating and the results are very promising.

There are a lot of young artists who might be a little short in the neck, or their legs might be not so perfect, or they have a little peculiarity in the construction of the body and they are rejected immediately in the ballet, classical ballet, whereas it is these elements which have more in them, you see; they can express much more than a line dancer.

That's very interesting because that's happened in recent years in drama; actors with irregular faces, or actors who speak an unorthodox English with the 'wrong' kind of accent, are now appearing in Shakespeare plays, who thirty years ago would not have been acceptable.

Well, that I'm glad to hear; that is new to me, but I have now every day experience in that. Now I am giving a diploma to three girls this year and, believe me, these girls, they probably won't be accepted in the ballet, but they say much more than any of the line dancers, and that opens the door to young people who love dancing, who *feel* dancing, and who can't do these wretched *muettes* and stand or turn on one leg, which is so sterile and inadmissible from the point of view of general art, general aesthetics. Classical ballet is a wonderful invention. Let it be a museum, let it be what it is, but don't educate young people in it. It is a grammar they must know, but from it there must spring something else, merging these elements – as I did in *Tricorne* a little bit, merging this strong Spanish technique with our forms.

And how much would you still want to accept the classical positions as a necessary vocabulary?

Well, look, all the things that touch motion, such as leaving the ground, obviously are the same; they are eternal, you can't do without them, you can't spring unless you have a certain élan which brings you from the first to the second elevation. These things will remain, you have to use them for dynamic, for crescendo of dynamic you have to do that; but you do that as a passing element when you want to whip something, you understand, and you go into something else – not standing dead in front of an audience, turning five times, stop and the applause comes. That is ridiculous. As elements of motion, classical dance is eternal. And the rest of their inventions are valid by intervals. To create curves, to create shapes – this is all valid – but not in the way it is frozen in classical ballet. 'You can do that' and 'You cannot do this'; such things are completely obsolete.

Now, would the kind of attitude to movement that you're talking about not imply that in the performance of a ballet there would be an almost inevitable need for improvisation? Do you think that those principles and that kind of freedom that you're talking about remain reconcilable with certain set movements which the dancer repeats at every performance?

Look, if we want to have some order and some intelligent approach to body motion, it must be precise. To that extent, like a pianist interpreting Beethoven might give an accent there, or do that or do that according to the style of the piece; like Wilhelm Kempff does, you see, but the thing must be precise; it must be written and it should not deviate from what's written, but the writing must be intelligent, the writing must not limit an artist; it must open the doors to him; to me it is an unshakeable principle. Improvisation in ballet is terrible . . . inadmissible.

WILLIAM COLDSTREAM 1962 and 1976

Two interviews recorded in London in April 1962 and October 1976. An edited version of the first was broadcast on the BBC Third Programme on 23 April 1962 and that version is published here for the first time. A substantial part of the text was incorporated into the interviewer's untitled catalogue introduction to the exhibition of William Coldstream, Anthony d'Offay Gallery, London, October–November 1976. That exhibition occasioned the second interview, which was broadcast on Radio 3 on 20 October. It was published in the *Burlington Magazine* for April 1977 and is reprinted here.

I

DAVID SYLVESTER *You paint more or less realistically, and always from nature. And you've painted people more than you have landscape or still life. I'd like to ask you why you choose to make most of your work as commissioned portraits? You have no economic need to do so because you can sell all of your output. And yet you seem to prefer this mostly as your choice of subject; apart from a few nudes, most of your paintings have been commissioned portraits. And I wonder if there is something peculiarly attractive to you about painting commissioned portraits?*

WILLIAM COLDSTREAM Yes, I think there is. I may say that I have sometimes very much enjoyed painting landscapes, but I've hardly ever painted a still life. One of the reasons I like painting portraits is that I'm interested in people; I like being with people. And the process of painting a portrait is really usually very enjoyable. You usually get to know someone well. And it is very interesting working there with them sitting there. One of the reasons one likes painting commissioned portraits, too – and I do like it – I'm not quite sure why I like it, but I should think one of the reasons is that it's rather nice to feel that someone really wants what you're going to do . . . you've got someone wanting you to paint. I think that's nice; and that's a help. And if you have great difficulty making yourself work, like I do, when the sitter's really going to arrive, you've jolly well got to be there and ready and paint, whether you feel like it or not. It's much more easy to put a model off that you're paying than to put a sitter off who one hopes is going to pay one. I think perhaps I enjoy, too, the narrowing down of the problem – that fewer choices are left to me. And I'm cornered into a problem which, although like all problems in painting is infinitely wide, in one sense appears to be narrower.

In what sense does it appear to be narrower?

Well, quite simply if you have someone who says, 'Will you paint my portrait?', and you say, 'Yes', and they say, 'When will you start?' and you say, 'Well, what about next Monday?', and they come, well, you know what you're going to do. You can't keep the man waiting all morning. So you ask him to sit down in a chair in the most comfortable position he can find, and the comfort of the sitter, to a large extent, dictates the pose, and you have to start painting before very long. But, if you're going to go to your studio and say, 'What am I going to do?', there seem so many alternatives that one's much slower getting started. But I admit that isn't anything to be proud of. I think that a great many purer and more talented painters than I always have had a very strong theme running in their head – like composers do, I think. Really talented painters and sculptors do tend to have some theme which is really obsessing them. And they will get on with it, whatever happens. I find – for whatever reason I don't know – I do find the presence of the person very interesting and perhaps that's a respectable and aesthetic reason, but boiling it down to more practical reasons, I know that if the person comes I've got to start painting.

Do you find that there are snags in painting somebody who commissions a portrait, and therefore tends to expect certain things of you which a model doesn't expect, don't these worry you?

Well, I've always found the sitters I've had have been extremely considerate. Mind you, I do warn them beforehand that I want a lot of sittings, so that they know what they're in for. But I have found that they have been pretty considerate, and they've been willing to go on sitting for a great many times. I don't like showing them the picture while I'm doing it, and they nearly always are extremely tactful about not asking to see it.

I think this shows great self-discipline on their part. How many sittings do you normally ask for?

Well, I reckon that I can't really produce anything that's got any way really under about sixty hours' work. And therefore I say, 'Well I'd like thirty sittings of two hours each, or I'll take it in sixty sittings of one hour. I can't do anything in under one hour.' But I don't mind having short sittings. Rather like starting straight in at the beginning of the hour. If you get a good sitter they'll sometimes sit straight through the hour and you work very intensively during that time, as you know that their time's at stake and you only have that hour. And I'm perfectly happy to break it up.

Let's say that you've done sixty hours' painting. Do you normally find you really like to go on very much more?

Yes, I think that usually I could go on a long way more. I'll tell you the thing that stops me going on, though, is once I've shown a picture to the sitter, I find it very difficult to go on, because supposing they like it – or at any rate don't dislike it too much, or say that something's nice about it – then you feel that when you've gone on they'll look at it and probably think it's not so nice, so that it somehow inhibits one. And I think that, while one's painting on a picture, it always seems to me that every time you start you've got to be willing to risk everything, and if there's a passage you happen to like, you always feel you've got to be prepared to put your brush right through it. You never have to have any regard for the past when you're painting. I think you've got to start work every time as though you are starting absolutely afresh, and risk everything. And the moment you feel, 'Well, I don't want to spoil this', you are well on the way to spoiling it. And, once you've shown it to a person, if they say there's something wrong with the mouth or the eyes or something, it's impossible to alter it, because I don't paint like that. I mean, the mouths and eyes, as it were, accrue – they're not put there, in my way of painting. And therefore I can't really do anything about the expression, as they say. So, even if I wish to, I can't really alter it to their requirements, so that's hopeless. And if they like it at all, or seem to, then I am rather afraid of spoiling it.

If they didn't see it . . .

But if they didn't see it, then I would . . . I think I could go on. Once I get interested in a thing, I think I could go on a very long time before I . . . I got bored.

Do you feel your pictures are unfinished?

Mmm, yes, I do. I'm not quite sure what finished means, but certainly finished means something carried a good deal further than most of my pictures.

Are there any of the paintings which you do feel are carried as far as they could go? That you feel that you wouldn't have known how to go on with them?

Well, not really. I think some of the pictures I wouldn't know how to go on with are some of the few pictures I've painted fairly quickly. There's a picture in the exhibition at Camberwell, a head of Miss Anrep, which I painted, I think, in a weekend. Well, I worked, you know, about six hours a day for three days and went straight through on the run, and then stopped. Well, I couldn't have taken that on. But that's not the sort of painting that I find comes naturally to me. I wish it did. I mean . . . but my painting is usually done by sort of short marches rather than one complete sweep. But if you do things in a complete sweep then the interruptions are impossible, and the continuation's impossible. You know what I mean.

The thing that struck me at the exhibition in looking at the whole progression of the work, the biggest difference between, say, 1937 and now was in the marks. There's some difference in the colour, which tends to be more raw now, and sometimes more vivid. But the big difference is in the marks. You don't any longer use this sort of hatching – this overall hatching all over the canvas – which you used in most of the earlier pictures. And I wondered if this difference in the marks was a purely technical matter or whether you felt it was the result of some difference in attitude towards the object?

I think it is due to some difference in attitude towards the object – everything's due to something. But of course it's tremendously difficult to know what one's own motives are. One's aware that one's changing, or one's aware after a period of time one's changed. But it's terribly difficult to really know a lot about oneself. I've often thought more recently that the marks are rather mannered and have, you know, thought I would try to suppress them more. But they seem to come like that. And I suppose I'm like most artists: once you start painting, you really haven't a lot of choice. I don't know if this is really true. But it seems to me that once you're embarked on a piece of work, you haven't a lot of choice. I mean the picture – I don't think it's a mystical thing to say, in a way; I think there are rational explanations – but the picture does seem to dictate what has to be done . . . though I mean I've been aware of many things – I mean I've been aware that my painting is naturally extremely inhibited and that sort of thing; I've made constant efforts, for instance, to sort of paint more freely or paint in a way which is sort of foreign to me. Then I tend always to be driven back somehow or other to the same way of painting.

But I suppose, or I hope, that it's a good thing to make these efforts to be unlike oneself in the hopes that in the long term one does broaden one's scope a bit. But I don't know whether that's true. I do, I must say, get great pleasure in actually touching the canvas and in the sort of configurations I'm making under the cloak of representing what I see. I'm very wary of dwelling on them too much because they would seem, if one did, to escape me, so I look back to the object. But there's no doubt that in any sort of painting if the thing seems to get going at all, one gets the extreme pleasure out of the actual configuration of marks that one finds oneself making. And if there seems to be a certain necessity about them, it's very satisfactory. Of course very often there isn't, and with a great many paintings one paints, they simply don't take.

Painting's rather like an inoculation, you know. I mean, you scratch the surface and you hope it'll take and swell up. But it doesn't always take, and you may try very hard or have been in very good form and the painting doesn't take, even though all the circumstances seem favourable. And then at other times, when circumstances seem very unfavourable, you feel it takes. I don't mean you think it's marvellously good, but at any rate you feel that within your own limits it's working.

What you've said about the marks suggests that it's not a question of your attitude to the object or any differing attitude to the object, but it is an attitude to your own posture as registered on the canvas. Obviously in the more recent works the handwriting is very conspicuous. In the earlier works it tended to be more self-effacing, with this even, overall hatching. But were you, even when making the even overall hatching, taking a certain pleasure in the particular texture this gave? Or, in other words, has your pleasure in the kind of marks you make come only when the marks became more free and more dissimilar?

Well, the pleasure has increased in the marks. I mean at . . . at a period in time when I was making every effort simply to try and make the whole thing look like what it does, and of course there are a great many qualifications for that, but I found it so terribly difficult – as I still do – that I was completely sort of absorbed in simply trying to get a thing in what I called the right place – whatever that may be. Well, I still take a lot of trouble about that. Though I know that, rationally speaking, it seems a rather ridiculous occupation. But I still do. But I do get much more pleasure now in actually marking the canvas. That sounds a frivolous occupation . . . (Laughs)

Well, that's painting, isn't it?

Well, I don't know.

But getting things in the right place: what role does measurement play in this?

Well, I think measurement is . . . I have to go back about measurement to my history. I've often thought, and I still often think, that I was singularly ill-equipped to become a painter – a thing which depressed me intensely when I was young – and I've thought probably I'd be much better if I'd taken up medicine or something; not that I'd necessarily be very good at it, but at any rate the results would be more certainly of some use. One of the things I had tremendous difficulty with at the Slade was in doing a representation of *anything*. I found that, whereas most of the students really could do what seemed to be magical drawings, which may not be very nice to look at but seemed to be exactly like the model, my things looked absolutely ridiculous and sort of childish. And after I left the Slade I determined, somehow or other, that I would learn to draw things which it never occurred to me to set myself to do. And I sat down and said, Well, how do you make the configuration on the canvas or piece of paper appear to be what is called 'look like'? And, if I reduce it to its very simplest terms, I've got arms and I must be able to stretch my arm out and put a series of marks which will do that. And that took enormous trouble, so that it is enormous trouble for me to represent anything. And in a way just trying to do this I find very entertaining. In a way, of course, it seems to me that probably, if one is being self-critical, it probably isn't any higher form of activity than trying to solve crossword puzzles. But I try and buoy myself up by feeling that there's some wider and more mystical significance attached to the activity that I really don't know.

I'm told you once said that you are interested in measurement because it gave you units of comparison. And that this was what you take to be the musical side of painting.

I think William Blake said, 'Bring out number, weight and measure in an age of dearth,' didn't he? I often say that to myself. But I am terribly interested in measurement, and no doubt there's a perfectly simple psychological explanation which could nowadays be entirely cleared up. But I *am* interested in measurement. I mean, if I walk down a street I often say, 'Now, how far is it to that lamp-post?'; and I will frequently pace it out – give myself a guess beforehand and see if I'm right or wrong. I get intense pleasure when I'm painting in just saying that this is two-thirds that, that is one-sixteenth more than that. Now, if you get a number of measurements, both on the surface of a canvas and then imagined measurements to some extent in depth working together, it gives you a kind of kick – I don't know why. And then this system builds up and you build onto it. I can't rationalise it. But it's a kind of play-acting, it seems, in a way, which gives one pleasure, somehow seems important. And then, of course, that side added to the other side – this configuration at the same time, having to do certain things in relation to what's called representation, those two activities together. And then there is the phenomenon of the sitter, which is quite different, which is not made of canvas or paint – which is an entirely different world – somehow related to these two other worlds: the so-called world of representation and then what is actually going on in this flat surface, which is nothing to do with either of them. The idea that somehow or other one's manipulating these three factors in one's mind is interesting. I'm afraid this sounds very pretentious, but that's the sort of thing that would go through my head.

You wouldn't be interested in measuring in the sense that Mondrian measured? You wouldn't be interested in the measurement of the canvas for its own sake?

Well, I've never been able to. When Victor Pasmore went over to abstract painting, I very much admired his first essays in abstraction, which made a great impression on me.

In 1947.

Yes. I did secretly several times try and engage my interests in dividing a canvas, dividing a plane up, you know, and that sort of thing. I could see that this was something which a person with the right sort of talent or sensibility could become absorbed in. To me it simply never took, because I felt I had to have something to do with representation in order for my interest to be engaged.

And when representing you always measure?

Well, I try very hard not to. But I'm always driven back to it because it seems to me to be extremely interesting to ascertain something. I know, of course, this is childish because the measurement in a sense is conventional. But the idea of making sure about the thing, within the limits of the game, means a lot to me.

You mean that you might for a while, during the course of a session, paint quite freely, then after a time find you have to measure and check?

Yes, yes, yes.

But you might paint freely for half an hour or more?

Yes. Not often, but certainly when I'm starting a painting I paint quite a long time freely without measuring now. But I am driven back to measuring.

Can you describe your technique of measuring?

Well, the technique of measuring is quite simple. It's the old idea: you look at what you're painting and you hold your pencil or brush out in the plane – in the picture plane, you see – and I say you put your hand . . . arm straight out and hold the brush up vertically and you mark off with one eye – as if you were shooting – a little bit. Of course it doesn't make sense; at least I'm told in any ordinary projection you can't really trust that and you can't use central perspective, for instance, in measuring like that. I mean if you're sitting seven or eight feet away from the model, you have a different picture plane when you're looking at the forehead from that in which you're looking at the knee. Because you look up or down, you don't look straight forward, so the thing doesn't really join up. It doesn't really make sense. But what I mean by measuring is quite literally holding a pencil up with one eye shut and marking a bit off on it.

When you're measuring you're using one eye; when you're painting without measuring you're using two eyes. Now, how can you square on the canvas, how can you reconcile, the results of what you do by measurement with what you do by looking two-eyed at the object?

You can't.

What happens as a result?

Well, you get something on the canvas and that gives you something to bite on. All this process, I suppose, in a way is to get something on the canvas which you can believe in – to get some knot of life or something going which will have some power of generating itself, you see. It seems less willed if you're measuring it. If you're trying to get something going by your own will-power, without reference to something that seems impersonal, it gives me a sense of distaste. If you have this rather sort of arbitrary thing, you feel the problem that's coming out is not one which you've been too much consciously associated with and therefore has that attraction. But I think this is all a very grand way of describing what hundreds of painters have often done.

But measurement is not a thing that can be carried out, as it were, systematically. I mean as it is, as you say, a knot. You can't . . . Would it be possible to paint . . . to do a painting altogether one-eyed and altogether as a complete system of measurement in this way?

Yes, I don't think it really matters whether you're painting with one eye or two eyes, you know. I don't think that makes a lot of difference. But if one supposes there is any aesthetic context in one's work, then I suppose you can say that all these processes, which are under the guise of being fairly rational, aren't really very reasonable; are simply rituals and methods of somehow getting one going. But of course any kind of making something in the artistic field can't be rationally described, at any rate by the marker. At least I don't know if it's ever been done. But I don't think so. One . . . the most aware painter, I think, isn't really quite certain of what they're doing or why they're doing it.

You want to make the thing, don't you, I think, as businesslike as possible? You don't want to start by thinking either in terms of self-expression or in terms of some canon of ideal beauty.

Yes, I suppose that's true. Yes.

You like the aesthetics to come in by the side door?

Yes. In the sense that I used to draw out of my head a great deal as a child. Throughout my childhood I drew a very great deal out of my head. I don't think the drawings were very talented, but I certainly drew a very great deal. But once I grew up and ever since I've found that what I draw out of my head, as it were, when there isn't a visual field of reference of a particular kind – that's to say when there isn't a subject, a concrete subject, which it is immediately related to – I dislike very much. I very much dislike the doodles I make when I'm telephoning. And when I am at a committee meeting it always seems other people's doodles look so much nicer than mine. I can't understand why mine don't. I've often thought, you know, it must be some way of moving the pencil so that one's doodle really does look nice. And how do the other people do it? But I have a certain horror of my own productions.

Before you went and worked in films, in documentary films, your painting was very influenced by Matisse.

Well, for a short time.

And when you came back to painting, you started painting these realistic pictures.

Yes.

Now, to what extent were you in this influenced by social ideas current at the time, to what extent on the other hand was it simply a sort of revulsion against the various kinds of painting that were then current – simply the desire to do something different, which after all is what generally tends to motivate painters in their style?

Well, I think for better or worse it was really a moral idea, however misguided. I had sort of Social Realist ideas in a sense that I would like to do something which – I would like to paint a sort of portrait which – people who might not know an enormous amount about painting would find interesting. I also got a kick out of trying to paint so-called realistic pictures when very few people were doing it. I mean there was the element of snobbism, I agree. But I realised too, because when I worked with Graham Bell, who carried these programmes to much greater extremes than I ever did – um – I realised too that if we were really going to try and carry out a programme of painting which should be more popular, to put it crudely, I soon realised I was singularly ill-equipped to do that because the first thing that a – any – popular painter needs (using popular in the good sense) is a very big visual vocabulary, that is to say a power to supply the imagination immediately with – with some kind of formula, do you see? And the power to illustrate; in fact, an illustrative power, which I was singularly lacking in.

At the time you wanted the paintings to have an appeal which would not be an aesthetic appeal, on the assumption that most people don't respond to what is specifically aesthetic in a painting, but that it would have, so to speak, a human interest?

Yes, that was in my mind. That was uppermost in my mind.

Do you still feel anything of that today?

No, much less. Things have turned out very differently from the way in which when I was young I thought they might turn out. You see, in the middle Twenties I would never have thought that painters like Picasso or Braque would have come to have what I think you could genuinely say, very great appeal. Not to everybody, but then not everybody likes football. But to an enormous number of people. And I think I underestimated the sort of aesthetic potential of what you could call large numbers of people, which I think was the tendency at the time: to think that, you know, that what was aesthetic – putting it crudely – was something that must be limited to a small number of people.

But is it? I mean, I can't speak for your views at the time; I can only speak for Graham Bell's, who published his views about the social thing – I mean, surely, the point was that the sort of people, I would have thought, who liked Picasso and Braque and abstract painters who are selling for large sums of money were representative of the kind of cultivated bourgeois taste that Graham Bell despised, and his point was reaching a genuinely mass public – some painting that would be of an interest to a mass public. And, although it's perfectly true that the milkman may be impressed that Picassos fetch such very large prices, and maybe because of that thinks there must be something in it – I don't think it's true that the majority of people actually like Picasso or find anything for themselves in it.

Oh well, not the majority, but it's very difficult to point to any popular activity of an aesthetic or sporting nature, as it were, that's to say of play nature, impractical nature, which the vast majority of people like.

But I – I do think that a very large number of people, who haven't spent a lot of time necessarily looking at pictures, do get much more pleasure than I would have thought they would have done at one time, out of these painters who one thought were very good, but were too obscure.

But would you still feel that you'd like your painting to have an interest and appeal for a large number of people?

Well, I suppose everyone would like their paintings to have an interest and appeal for a large number of people, but that is not a thing which now really weighs with me.

At what time did this tend to disappear?

Gradually.

In point of fact, you're really an exceptionally uncompromising painter, an exceptionally private painter. I think most observers would tend to feel this. It was certainly felt by the people who sent back your portrait of the Bishop of Chichester, because the likeness wasn't sufficiently pleasing. From which it's clear that in practice you paint very much for yourself – as much as anybody.

I think it is an awfully difficult question as to who a person paints for. I've never really gone into it or thought it out carefully, but I would tend to say off the cuff that all artists really paint for themselves. I don't believe there are many artists, if any, who quite sort of deliberately set out to make a recipe of what will be pleasing or required. I think it's very unusual. I would think it very eccentric.

Do you think that in the 1930s, when you – to some extent – and Graham Bell to an extreme extent, had this idea of doing a kind of popular painting, it was really a kind of sense of guilt about doing a – an unnecessary activity?

Yes, very much so, I think, yes. I think it was. No doubt it was slightly puritanical. And I think if I'd had a greater amount of talent, in a way, of course that would have outweighed it. But if one has enormous difficulty in doing something, then the objections to it of course weigh more easily than if one hasn't. (Laughs)

II

How do you feel about being a full-time painter at long last?

I retired, as you know, from the Slade a year ago exactly. Before that I had been painting a good deal, but I very much enjoy having the whole of my time for painting. I was rather afraid beforehand that I would find it difficult to do that, but I have surprised myself by really enjoying painting every day and painting quite a lot.

Now that you are painting every day, how many paintings do you tend to have on the go simultaneously?

Well, I usually have about four because I don't like painting for very long on any one picture. About three hours is about as much as I can work on one picture at a stretch, and I rather like having a day or two in between so as to come back to the picture fresh.

Do you ever feel any temptation to paint out of your head?

No. Of course, when I first started as a student I painted out of my head, but I more and more felt completely disgusted with the results and I really haven't tried to do it for many years.

In what circumstances have you tried painting out of your head?

Oh, I haven't for a long time now. It wouldn't be able to hold my attention. I wouldn't feel I knew what to do.

And you've never, for example, having done a drawing, wanted to work from that?

Yes, I have, but then it has always seemed to be that all I'm doing is to try and reproduce the drawing, which doesn't seem to have much point. I know that most of the great paintings of the world are certainly done out of people's heads or from drawings, so I hold no brief with this point of view. I'm merely saying it is the case with me.

Yes, indeed. I wasn't assuming that you were arguing it as a sort of position, but I wonder if you can say why it is that it bores you to paint from a drawing rather than to do the actual painting from the model or the motif.

Well, I suppose that as a student I had very strong feelings of inferiority about my own skill in drawing both from things and out of my head. It seemed to me that I was much worse at it than fellow-students, which is not false modesty. I had extraordinarily little facility. I think I had possibly some facility with manipulating paint, but very little facility in representing anything. I did a lot of drawing as a child and used to get prizes at school. They were always imaginative things. I never had sat down and drawn from anything until well into my Slade career, when I suddenly decided I would like to try and do it, but I was always aware that I was not at all good at drawing either from things or out of my head and I used to get very fed up with the results. It was after I had been at the Slade for about a year that I suddenly for the first time thought I would really look at something very closely and see what happened if I responded to it very strictly, and this began to fascinate me. It seemed to me that the results that I got down gave me a certain satisfaction which was quite different in kind from anything I did out of my head, and really from that time onwards I always worked looking at something and trying as it were to represent it, whatever one means by that.

But you have made attempts to do the other thing?

Not for many years. I mean, in the old days of Objective Abstraction when my friends Rodrigo Moynihan and Geoffrey Tibble were doing paintings I much admired which really were totally abstract and rather before their time, in the early Thirties, I made many attempts to do that, but I found that the results seemed inept and did not hold my attention.

I think, for example, that I have known cases of a painter doing a work from the model and then doing from memory another or other versions which were started off by the first painting and possibly feeling that away from the model they could make the thing more like, or more what they were trying to do. How is it that you haven't felt any temptation to do that?

When I start a painting, I don't think I have any intention; that is to say, I don't say that I want it to be like this or like that. I work and see what happens, really; so that I haven't got a sort of goal, as it were. I want to see what accrues as I paint.

So it is almost inevitable that you can only return to the model all the time.

And there is a sense I feel in painting strictly from the model that somehow it has less to do with oneself than if one is painting out of one's head. I have a feeling that there is a certain kind of impersonal quality – which may be illusory. I have a feeling there's a certain impersonal quality one can get if one works very strictly, objectively as it were, from nature, which doesn't happen to my work if I'm working out of my head, and this somehow pleases me. I feel that it is something that is detached from me and that I'm not too personally involved. Now, I don't suppose that makes sense in any serious philosophical terms, but I'm merely saying these are the sorts of ideas which would occur to me.

Well, it certainly makes sense in psychological terms. But you might get the same kind of result by painting from photographs. Only, you've never done that either, have you?

No. Well, of course, in photographs the sporting element is missing. I mean, it's too much like shooting a sitting bird isn't it? I mean, the thing is, if you are painting from a landscape or painting a model, you don't really know what you are looking at. You know what you are looking at less than if you look at a photograph. If you look at a photograph you have the thing formulated, but looking at a landscape or looking at any scene in front of you, it's not on the flat. It is a very, very complex phenomenon that one is faced with and it seems to me much more inscrutable than a photograph.

What it comes down to is that really the interest for you is unravelling the inscrutable?

Yes, you're dealing with something that seems infinite and not in any simple way definable, even in the kind of algebra one uses to express it.

Would I be right in inferring from that that one of the most exciting problems for you is this translation which you've got to do unaided of what is in space into something flat?

Yes, I think that is true. I think one has a feeling that certain colours put together represent greater or less distances away, and so forth. How much they really do, I don't know, but one builds up a whole system in one's mind about what should stand for what and how one could somehow make things stand further or nearer and this and that and the other, and one gets a system going on canvas prompted by the so-called facts which one is looking at, and it builds up a certain autonomous quality in itself and, at the same time, one keeps referring to what one's looking at.

That problem must excite you very much, because by always painting from the model there are a great many subjects that you can never hope to deal with. I mean Degas was able to deal with certain subjects by using photographs of figures in movement. Or Cézanne, by going and doing sketches of the soldiers bathing by the river, was able to come back and make up compositions of female bathers with figures in movement. You're prepared to forego all that because you want to keep this involvement with translating what is spatial into something flat.

Well, I suppose that may be true partly. But, as I find it very difficult to do people standing still, I haven't got to the stage of them moving about, so I've got quite a lot to go on with.

Well, as you know, one may be able to get away with things more easily with people moving about.

I do get terribly interested in a fairly limited subject-matter and once I have started I feel, you know, that it's infinitely difficult and complicated, so that I don't feel that I've got to the end of anything.

Now, it's interesting that you say that about getting to the end of anything. Because quite a number of painters from nature – Rembrandt is an obvious example; Velázquez, though in his case it may have been because he was employed to do so; certainly Giacometti – paint the same person over and over again feeling that there's no end to painting the same person. Really, as Giacometti said, one could use the same model all one's life. Now, with yourself, I know there are a few cases where you have done two or three paintings of the same model, but on the whole you don't constantly return to the same model. Would you like to?

Yes, I would rather, but it's difficult to get people; it's not easy to get models in the sense that, if you are not painting all day every day, you can hardly offer someone employment with continuity. It's not easy to get people for certain if they are only coming casually two or three times a week, so you can't always get the same person. That's merely a practical thing. And if one was very well off, I suppose, one would offer a personal retainer to use them, but I mean on the whole that's not too sensible, so that's just a practical matter. I mean there are one or two models I would be perfectly happy to go on painting.

There is, for example, this girl of whom you are now on your third painting.

Well, she sits very well because she has two little children to take to school every day and she just comes and sits for me while they are at school and then collects them, so she doesn't mind if she doesn't come every day – that makes a good arrangement.

There's a characteristic in your work which has become more and more pronounced as the years have gone by, and this is the increasing visibility of the marks in which you record on the canvas the measurements that you make in painting. In the early works, in the Thirties, the measurement marks were almost invisible, they were covered by the paint, by the representational brush marks. I think it was in one or two of those paintings that you did of Indian soldiers during the war that they began to become more visible, and they have been doing so more and more – you are more and more inclined to leave them uncovered.

That's not intentional. I hadn't noticed it particularly until you pointed it out. It's not intentional; I don't mean them to be showing through. In fact now that you have said it, I think I will try and not show them so much.

1962 and 1976

Oh, dear. But one so much enjoys looking at them. I wish I hadn't said anything.

It is really like having one's shirt hanging out.

But you must have been aware that you were leaving them there?

No, not terribly, no. I think if, when one is making something, the marks of the work are left behind, it's annoying if they become self-conscious, one parades them. I think it's all right if they are a genuine by-product. I don't know why, but I feel it's not a good idea to make a virtue of leaving traces of one's method.

Well, I don't think there is any feeling of that, I must hasten to say. I do think it's a matter of leaving one's shirt out, because one is so involved in what one is doing that one's shirt slips out and one is too busy to notice this. But I wonder why it's been slipping out more and more.

Perhaps one gets less cautious about the way one works as one gets older. But what is interesting is the way that one's work changes without one being aware of it. A little while ago I thought I would try and paint a picture exactly like I painted, or as I thought I painted, thirty years ago. And it's quite impossible. Just for fun I tried to see if I could do exactly as I used to. I couldn't, of course. It's quite understandable that one can't, but I mean it's strange, isn't it? Because the sort of changes in one's work are not things one is aware of and the way one thinks one's developing or progressing or regressing or whatever it is, is not the way in which things really are. One doesn't really know the direction one's work is taking until a long time afterwards.

Of course, maybe the increasing visibility of the brush marks is related to the fact that in the later work there's a much greater degree of variation in how far different parts of the painting are realised. I mean, in the Euston Road days, there was a fairly uniform mark, which is certainly very far from being the case now.

Yes.

49

But in your work how much going over is there?

Oh, there's no going over. I mean I never rub out. I just gradually build up. I like to feel that the whole surface in a way is sort of coming along together up to a point. It isn't that I don't work sometimes a very long time in one corner but I like to feel that the whole surface is remaining somehow in balance at any moment. That's to say, I don't like to feel there's a hole in the canvas, so I like it to be even and to grow evenly.

Do some parts tend, though, in spite of that to get ahead of other parts?

Oh yes, they do, they do. When one starts painting every day, one just has a strong feeling that this is what you need to do, you don't really quite know why, but you feel you've got to do this bit.

Do you find in painting a nude that the face interests you as much as it does when you're painting a portrait?

Oh yes, very much so. I think the face in relation to the whole figure obviously has a special meaning when you see it in the context of the whole figure. I would not find it very interesting on the whole to paint a torso for instance without the head. I think, in the case of people with their clothes off, there are all sorts of things which strike one that are rather moving – the sort of weathering of the face compared with the more covered white body and all those sorts of things. And people's faces tend to age rather differently, or one appears to think they age rather differently, than figures often. At any rate, I think the face with its tremendous concentration of expression compared with the less expressive body is very interesting, because of course the human face is something to which one is tremendously responsive; one can tell from a long way away what a person is focusing at, one can recognise their expression, by tiny movements; and the face therefore is much more concentrated in the signals it gives than the figure, on the whole, because one's much less used to looking at the figure. One doesn't read the figure in the way that one reads the expression in the face and therefore you have this tremendously concentrated and expressive focal point, yet indissolubly attached to the figure – somehow it's a piquant contrast which I think is moving and interesting.

What brings a painting to a stop?

Time. With most of the paintings I've done I think I feel I ought to have gone on with them. I could go on; whether I'm right in supposing they'd be any better I don't know, but I feel that I could go on a long way and I usually stop out of expediency because I feel I can't make a person sit any longer or, you know, something like that. Really on the whole I feel I could go on for a very long time anyway. I mean it's a sort of open-ended thing.

Nevertheless, there is a moment of decision when you feel that you're going to leave it, that's it; except of course when it becomes impossible for the model to go on sitting, which does often happen. But there must be many occasions when you know that the person could have gone on; there was no particular reason for stopping. But you stopped.

Sometimes laziness (I suppose one ought to have gone on) and of course sometimes the feeling that one must produce a certain number of pictures. It's getting too much of a good thing if you paint one picture in two or three years. You've got to, from a common-sense point of view, have a little more output than that.

Does it get more difficult as you go on?

No, it doesn't get more difficult provided you always paint as though you were starting. What's fatal is to try and finish a picture. If I feel that a picture is required by a certain date or something, I become completely inhibited because I feel that, when you paint, you must, every time you take the work up, you must risk the whole thing and be prepared to sacrifice what may seem to you the most successful piece. You can't paint with savers, you've got to risk the whole thing. So if there's any question of having to have it ready by a certain moment one either just leaves it and says, 'Well, have it like it is' or one goes on with it and says, 'I can't tell you when I can finish.'

Of course this is most likely to happen with a commissioned portrait.

No, not really. I mean, my sitters are nearly always people who have some idea of what they're in for and they tend to be extremely decent about sitting.

Nevertheless you've been doing many fewer commissioned portraits in the last few years.

Well, I find it very difficult to get people to sit because I've got to say to them nowadays: I don't think you're likely to get anything worthwhile having under thirty or forty sittings. And naturally people haven't got that time, so that it's only the unusual person who is prepared to do it.

Do you know why it is that up till 1950 you'd done very few paintings of the nude? I think that your nudes are on the whole your greatest paintings, and a high proportion of your work has been of a nude in recent years. But you took a very long time to come round to it. As far as I remember, I can only remember one painting of a nude of yours before 1950.

Well, of course I was appointed to run the Slade in 1949 and there are lots of nudes in art schools, you know. I didn't use the school models, but I met a lot of models and so it was easy for me to get models to come there because in the days when I first was Slade professor in '49 we were employing sixteen models a day; and of course I knew a lot of models and had plenty of choice and could get them to come and sit for me at odd times and also had a very nice warm studio, so that really is partly a practical thing, I think.

It's very interesting the way in which you attempt to come back to saying that it is something practical or something expedient which has determined what you do.

Well, I think a great many things are determined by expediency or at any rate by perfectly prosaic things, aren't they?

This tends to be the case and yet, on the other hand, there are, one might say, quite a number of artists who bully circumstances into fitting in with them. Do you think that your acceptance of expediency is part of the same attitude as makes you choose to work from the model so that something always tends to be imposed from outside, so that you see what happens? You accept what is there whether it's the case of the appearance of a specific thing, a specific place, a specific person; you also accept what is there in the sense of circumstance, and you adapt your working methods to circumstance.

I suppose up to a point that is true, yes, but I don't think there's anything mysterious about it. Everyone does that, don't they, up to a point?

I would have thought that you do it a lot more than most people.

Really? Well, I like painting given subjects rather than imposing. For instance, if I'm painting a portrait I wouldn't try and make the person sit in any particular attitude which I'd thought about beforehand. I would always take the view that the best thing to do is to sit them down in the most comfortable position, that there is a solution to every problem and that therefore, provided the person's comfortable, you know, one attitude is as good as another. I wouldn't have ideas about it.

But it does seem to interest you very much to try to deal with things as they are rather than to set things up to suit.

Yes it does, it does. I would feel a bit inhibited about arranging a still life or something very carefully. This is pure superstition, of course; one arranges it all the time. But the fact is I would like to take things as they seem to me as little affected by me first as possible.

Cézanne, for example, when he was doing a still life, would use coins to shift the position, say, of an apple, in order to bring it into a slightly different position to that in which it would naturally sit on a table or a plate. He'd wedge a coin underneath, starting the painting, as it were, before he started painting.

Well, that wouldn't be in my book of rules, that's against the rules.

Yes. My very favourite among your paintings is one in the present exhibition of a nude lolling back in an armchair, which was painted in the room which had been Adrian Stokes's drawing-room. And, just behind this girl, you've dealt with this, it seems to me, rather awkward cumbersome shape of Adrian Stokes's radiogram which you've left there in the picture as something to deal with. There it was, the furniture in the room, and it seems to me, as a non-painter, that it must have presented quite an awkward compositional problem. Did you quite consciously decide, as a matter of principle, on not messing about with things, or not interfering?

Yes. Because I didn't want to move the furniture too much, and, you know, the girl came and I just sat her down, and I thought: well, this is the real situation; she's sitting for me in this room, obviously she's a model, sitting for me to paint her in this room and there it is; that's the situation. I'll see what I can do with it.

Did it enter your head to shift the radiogram?

It was very heavy.

Expediency again. But did it actually, while you were painting, present difficulties?

No. I just thought: what an extraordinary thing to paint this radiogram; and what on earth am I doing painting a radiogram behind a lady with her clothes off at nine o'clock in the morning? So I thought – there it is, that's the situation; we go on.

I think what you've been really saying all the time is that what interests you is this challenge of dealing with what is there.

Yes.

And that you don't want to take any shortcuts whether it's the use of photographs or something else.

No. It's partly a game, you know.

54

1962 and 1976

In which the rules are going to be jolly difficult.

No. The rules are very complicated, but one has these rules, everyone has rules all the time they live, really. Of course, as you were saying, every action one performs is partly explicable through utilitarian motives and things; but also there's usually a big undertone of unconscious appendages to the way you cross the road or how you mount the stairs or anything, isn't there? And there's a double meaning to all the things we do: there's the practical one and there are the imponderable undertones. An action may contain symbolism to a person in all sorts of ways, don't you think? And, of course, the double meaning has become very important in those games which are called art.

KEN ADAM 1999 and 2001

This is in two parts. The first is the introductory note written for the exhibition catalogue *Moonraker, Strangelove and other celluloid dreams: the visionary art of Ken Adam*, co-authored by Ken Adam and David Sylvester, published by the Serpentine Gallery, 1999. It is followed by an interview recorded in 2001.

I

There are moments in film where the set is more magnetic than the actors, the dialogue, the editing, the music. Some of the unforgettable sets are real places: the Odessa Steps, Monument Valley, the rolling streets of San Francisco. Some are made up: 'Tara' in *Gone With the Wind*, the 'Silver Sandal' nitery in *Swingtime*, 'Xanadu' in *Citizen Kane*, the Pentagon war-room in *Dr Strangelove*. (Perhaps this latter locus too should have been designated inside quotation marks: it's said that, when Ronald Reagan came to Washington as the newly elected President, he asked to be taken to see the Pentagon war-room he had seen in the film, a holy-of-holies he wanted to view in the round, being innocent – despite his long experience as a movie actor – of the fact that it had never existed outside Shepperton Studios.) But who were the individuals who dreamt up the architecture of such sets? We can read quite informative histories of the cinema without coming upon their names, though some of them have left a mark on the medium as individual and as deep as those of great actors, directors, writers or cinematographers. But they somehow tend to share the anonymity of the designers of legendary monuments: Grand Central Station, Wembley Stadium, the Sacré Coeur, the White House.

Film designers are generally known as 'art directors'; for some time it was 'unit art directors', in distinction to 'supervising art directors', the ones who ran the studio art departments and received the prizes won by their subordinates. The creator of the room Reagan wanted to see, Ken Adam, was credited as 'art director' on his early films as head designer; since 1957, 'production designer' has been his usual credit. It is a term which seems to have been invented by David O. Selznick when producing *Gone With the Wind*. In a famous memorandum written in 1937 on the subject of the use he wanted to make of William Cameron Menzies – that great cinematic figure who was not only a designer but had directed such films as *Things to Come* – he contended that *G.W.T.W.* needed someone of Menzies's talent and experience so that the film could be prepared almost down to the last camera angle before shooting started. The whole physical side of the film should be personally handled by one man who had little or nothing else to do. Menzies's participation would therefore be 'a lot greater in scope than is normally associated with the term "art direction". Accordingly I would probably give him some such credit as "Production Designed by William Cameron Menzies" . . .'

Giving this amount of responsibility to the designer of a film was not a total break with the past, more a difference of degree: traditionally the job of art director could be purely architectural or could include involvement in creating story boards and suggesting camera angles; there was always a tendency for the art director to do some directing of the action. At the same time, the job of the 'production designer' is not often as comprehensive as Menzies's was on *G.W.T.W.* That is to say, this credit is like all credits for collaborative work in that its precise meaning tends to vary from one project to another. (In one of the projects in which Adam was involved in an especially personal way, *Pennies from Heaven*, his role in designing the production got an odd pair of credits: 'associate producer' and 'visual consultant'.)

As it happens, William Cameron Menzies (pronounced as it is spelt) was to play a critical role in Adam's career. By the time they met, Adam, born in 1921, had worked in England or Italy on such films as *The Queen of Spades* (1948, directed by Thorold Dickinson), *Captain Horatio Hornblower R.N.* (1950, Raoul Walsh), *The Crimson Pirate* (1952, Robert Siodmak) and *Helen of Troy* (1955, Robert Wise). At this point Mike Todd invited him to work on *Around the World in Eighty Days* (1956, Michael Anderson) as one of two art directors operating under the command of Menzies. Not surprisingly, the great man became a mentor and an ongoing source of inspiration. Adam was assigned the sets for the film's European loci, and among those he created were his first masterpieces – Lloyd's of London, with its challenging use of black and white, and the employment bureau, with its chorus of candidates for jobs placed in a very straight line while John Gielgud bickers with a bewigged Noël Coward. There is no knowing how far this surge of inventiveness and wit was due to Menzies's influence, how far to a simple process of maturation, how far to the spur of Todd's outrageous tycoonery. But it is certain that Adam had now made it clear that he was already the most brilliant and masterly designer in British films.

This meant that he got invited to work under several top American directors when they came over to make a film in Britain. He worked under John Ford on *Gideon's Day* (perhaps the worst of all Ford's bad films), under Robert Aldrich on *Ten Seconds to Hell*, *The Angry Hills* and *Sodom and Gomorrah*, and under Jacques Tourneur on Night of the Demon, aka *Curse of the Demon* (1957). This is a gem of a horror film by a master of the genre, based on a story by another, M. R. James. Sadly, it was left flawed by the interference of thick-headed producers who demanded blatancy where Tourneur and Adam would have preferred suggestion: thus, whereas the director and still more the designer wanted the Demon to be manifest only in glimpses of its great steaming footprints, the producers insisted on two appearances of the monster in person and Adam had to come up with a toothy cousin of King Kong.

The next major step in Adam's progress was constrained in another way: *The Trials of Oscar Wilde* (1960, Ken Hughes) had an extremely limited budget, but Adam contrived to make a shining aesthetic virtue out of practical necessity. The *réclame* won for this film did much to get him the job that made him a star: designing the first of the James Bond films, again on a small budget, *Dr No* (1962, Terence Young). And this triumph in turn induced Stanley Kubrick to hire him for *Dr Strangelove or: How I Learned to Stop Worrying and Love the Bomb* (1963). This was undoubtedly the finest film he was ever to work on. But he did work on at least one other black comedy that was outstandingly well-scripted and well-acted, *Sleuth* (1972), made by another top American director, Joseph L. Mankiewicz, and the two films are perfect models of antithetic ways in which the settings and scripts in black comedies can interact. In *Strangelove* the war-room set, while preposterous in its extravagance, is also seriously imposing and reflects the awesomeness of the tragic plot; the absurdity and subversiveness of the dialogue are a hysterically funny foil to the sense of doom. *Sleuth*, on the other hand, is a drawing-room comedy in which, although the situations deal in life and death, they are essentially flip, and the sets are a continuous active ingredient in the fun.

Strangelove and *Sleuth* are also complementary in that one represents Adam as a designer on a heroic scale, the other as a designer on a more domestic scale. Others among his more intimate works are the interiors in *Agnes of God* (1985, Norman Jewison), which recall Vermeer in their sober, silent greys and blacks and whites and the severe rectangles of the doorways and corridors and grilles, and the aborted recent project for a stage production of Alban Berg's opera, *Wozzeck*.

But it was, of course, the epic architecture that Adam created in the 1960s and '70s for *Strangelove* and the Bond films that made his reputation. Among his seven Bond films, his finest achievements seem to me to be *You Only Live Twice* (1967), *The Spy Who Loved Me* (1977) and *Moonraker* (1979). It may or may not be relevant that these were the three Bond films which were directed by Lewis Gilbert. It is certainly relevant that two of them were the last two of the seven. In the course of an interview at the time of *Moonraker*'s release, Adam told Eliot Wald: 'The producers no longer really use the Ian Fleming novels. We start with a general story-line, which is almost always the same lately. Then we go location scouting, looking for places that haven't been seen in the movies too much. On the trip, the director, the writer and I begin putting together concrete ideas . . . The Bond films are done so loosely that the script isn't the Bible that it is in most films. It changes all the time and the whole process of writing it is like some democratic debating society.' This was really Adam's modest and diplomatic way of telling the truth that what really mattered in these films was what he contributed: what are probably the most amazing and enthralling pieces of fantastic architecture in the history of talking pictures. They might even have been surpassed if the sketches he made in the late 1970s for a proposed but aborted translation to the cinema of *Star Trek* had been realised: these extraordinary visions, incidentally, sometimes seem to anticipate the architecture of Daniel Libeskind.

This brief note is not the place for serious investigation of possible origins or antecedents for Adam's architectural imaginings, but I would offer one suggestion. Adam is an avowed fan of Piranesi, and it is easy to see an affection for the *Carceri*, especially, in a number of his sketches. But Piranesi's vision tends to be hairy and Adam's to be bald, Piranesi's to be Roman and Adam's to be Egyptian, and I suspect that among Piranesi's heirs in France there was one visionary architect with whom Adam has a closer while surely unconscious affinity: Étienne-Louis Boullée (1728–99). One of the significant features that Adam's work shares with Boullée's is its awesome use of vast spheres, sublime incarnations of the form of which

Boullée wrote: 'From whatever side we look at this shape, no trick of perspective can alter the magnificence of its perfect form . . . Of all bodies, it offers the largest surface to the eye, and this lends it majesty. It has the utmost simplicity because that surface is flawless and endless. Besides these qualities, we must speak of a grace that owes its being to an outline that is as soft and as flowing as it is possible to imagine.' Boullée's *Newton's Cenotaph*, for example, or his *Conical Cenotaph*, its apex truncated, cypresses around its base and a huge hemisphere within, present a world very close to Adam's.

The failure of the Bond and *Strangelove* designs to win a single Oscar would be astonishing were it not for the fact that Oscar awards have always been aberrant: after all, John Wayne himself failed to get one for *Red River* or *Hondo* or *The Searchers* and had to wait till, with one foot in the grave, he had one kindly conferred upon him for True Grit. By the same token, Adam's only Oscars were awarded in 1975 and 1994, both for atypical work, on *Barry Lyndon* and *The Madness of King George*, costume dramas which exhibit all his marvellous talent for pastiching or quoting historic architecture but not his more important talent for inventing fantastic architecture. Nevertheless, King George is a wonderful film, and Adam's contribution to it is wonderfully resourceful and convincing in the ways it mixes existing and constructed sets – as in the series of scenes in which the King hijacks the harpsichord at an orchestral concert, wrestles the Prince of Wales to the ground, and flees with his young children up a stone spiral staircase to escape the delusory threat of rising floods. Totally constructed interiors are interspersed with the Painted Room at Greenwich, a staircase in St Paul's, and part of a roof at Arundel Castle to which Adam added tall stone chimneys whose resemblance to classical columns would evoke the tragic.

Adam's brilliance in both appropriating and pastiching bits of the eighteenth century is almost matched when he is dealing with biblical times, as in *King David* (1985), or with yesterday, as in *Pennies from Heaven* (1981), the musical scripted by Dennis Potter and directed by Herbert Ross, a close friend of Adam's with whom he has worked on seven films. Here the evocation of Chicago in the 1930s is entirely fabricated, using no photography of real places (with the notable exception of a long road across a flat landscape which bears a striking resemblance to the road where Cary Grant was ambushed by an aeroplane in *North by Northwest* –

and is indeed that very road, near Los Angeles). By the same token, while the songs, including their performances, are lifted from period recordings, the dances are pastiches subtle enough to contain comment as well as imitation – which is what makes this a Postmodernist musical. Thus the dazzling parody of a Busby Berkeley number is not just a re-creation but an updating, so that there is suddenly a passage where the chorus and its reflection at a lower level anticipates the layered horizontal rhythms of photographs taken in the 1990s by Andreas Gursky.

Pennies from Heaven may provide a key to the essential nature of Adam's more spectacular designs: that in spirit they are designs for musicals. In *Around the World in Eighty Days* the row of job candidates in the employment bureau has the look of a chorus line. In Goldfinger the fight to the death in Fort Knox between Bond and the Korean hired assassin, Odd-Job, is as balletic as it is violent. If Salon Kitty is one of the few films ever made in which orgiastic scenes are not unintentionally comic, it is because of the choreographic art with which nude and semi-nude figures disport themselves among Nazi banners. In The Madness of King George there are frequent surging movements of human figures – sometimes a small group, sometimes a crowd, as when the court has assembled for the concert – which are highly balletic. And again and again in the Bond films there are choruses of rapt figures moving like dancers, above all in the scenes in *Moonraker* in which the beautiful young couples who are to be the progenitors of a master race are parading through the halls and corridors of a space station like the chorines of the great Hollywood musicals of the 1930s, films which, hardly less than the UFA productions of Ken Adam's native country, must have formed a large part of his early boyhood intake of celluloid dreams.

II

DAVID SYLVESTER *I've been doing interviews for fifty years, Ken, and this is the first time that I've ever been able to say to a victim: when we were at prep school together, it was obvious what field you were going to work in, and you did. But of course, we knew at school that you were going to be something in the visual arts. But you didn't think of becoming a painter or a sculptor . . .?*

KEN ADAM No, at that stage, no. When I was, what, fifteen years old, I liked to draw and I liked to paint and I liked to work with my hands, but I really didn't know which way to go. But, shortly after that, a young Hungarian painter was staying at my mother's boarding house in Hampstead, who was a friend of the Kordas, and through Vincent Korda he changed to become a cameraman – one of the first to be trained in technicolour photography. He became the first sort of technical cameraman, and he introduced me to Vincent Korda and showed me the studios, I think it was Denham in those days. And I said, 'Well, you know, this would interest me' and Korda said, 'Well, before you even think about it you should get, I would suggest, some architectural background. Because I think you've got to know about design and history of architecture, and art.' And that's more or less when I decided that was my future, but I wasn't sure – I think I preferred film to the theatre but I was always, sort of, permutating between the two possibilities.

Ah-ha. The other day, I watched some clips from some of your films, and at the end of it I said to myself: if I'd been Ken watching this, I might say, 'Well, I see I've created a world, I see I've created a world.' If I was an architect watching a film about cities I'd built – you'd have had the same feeling that this was a world that you'd created. Do you feel, looking back on your life, glad that you did work in film and that you didn't become an architect and build real rather than imaginary places?

Yes. Oh, there's no doubt. I mean, I never would have liked to build permanent structures, and also all the problems, you know, the practical problems with architecture bored me. So I had to almost release myself from the discipline of an architectural study to express myself in films, because though very often one is called a film architect, basically you design for the camera, and that is where the big difference comes. And my first problem, when I started as a draughtsman at Twickenham and at Riverside Studios, was to learn as much of the elementary, or the basic, principles of film design, designing for the camera and so on. And then I spent certainly two or three years learning the craft and thought this was relatively easy – I also managed to release myself from the discipline of architecture and express myself much more theatrically. Not for the sake of being theatrical, but because I felt I could achieve settings which are more suitable for the dramatic impact of the scene, by departing from reality and sort of creating a little bit of my own reality. And that I think has paid off, in many pictures, and strangely enough, David, you know that one sometimes is criticised for designing these lavish decors for the Bond films – with the possibility of the actor being overpowered by the sets. But my experience, right up to the latest picture I've done, is that actors like Harvey Keitel or Steve Martin have come to me and thanked me for making them feel completely at home. So, you know, the set was created really for them and that's a great compliment.

When you first started to become involved in film design, was there a particular kind of movie to which you were drawn? Did you have any feeling that you might like to do comedy, or costume, or horror? Was there any particular field or fields in which you felt that you especially wanted to work?

Not really, no. Because I think one was very happy to get a film, of course, and so I was not yet in a position to be choosy. And I really tried to deal with every type of film. I mean, I was brought up in the sort of major big American productions in Italy in the Fifties, you know, like *Helen of Troy* and *The Crimson Pirate*, and the Flynn picture, *The Master of Ballantrae*, so I learnt the way Hollywood worked, and those big costume period pictures did appeal to me. And then I took everything – you know, small pictures in England – and I also like to design, or try my hand at designing, Georgian interiors and that kind of period appealed to me. The first time I really started being more critical about screenplays was when I first worked for Bob Aldrich, who was a great American director and a great person. We were going to make a picture in England, actually, called *Ten Seconds to Hell*, and then we made it in Berlin in 1957/8, and I was looking through my notes the other day, as he's unfortunately no longer with us, but he said later that what impressed him about me was, on our first meeting when we were driving to a studio and he was explaining the script to me and I said, 'Well, Bob, yes, I agree with you, but for me there are really two separate stories.' I was very young at the time and he didn't agree with me – but about ten or fifteen years later he wrote, you know: 'Who was this arrogant young man who had the chutzpah to criticise my script?' And really, from that time onwards I was equally interested in the story and sometimes felt how visually I could improve on the story. And so I worked very closely, as a whole, with the director, and sometimes a writer and so on. I really wanted to be totally involved with the making of film. Then, as time went on, I became more choosy about the subject-matter. Also, the important thing is not so much that you get an interesting script, but that you work with a good or great director, because it's such a collaborative art form making films, and if you have a great relationship with the director, and hopefully the cameraman too, then you're there, the battle's won, you can really function properly.

But the curious thing is that your greatest creations have not necessarily been those working with the great directors, like Kubrick and Bernardo, but often with relatively minor directors. One could say you were the author, more than the director: that the films were your creation. That, it's an old cliché now: who is Bond? Is Bond Sean Connery? No, Bond is Ken Adam. In other words – let's look at the Bond films for a moment as a separate category – the Bond films are Ken Adam films in a way that a Hitchcock film is a Hitchcock film. You are the main creative force in those films. The unforgettable thing about them, the thing that has imprinted the films upon our consciousness, is your vision; it's more you than either Sean Connery or Ian Fleming. You know, I watched Intolerance *the other day . . . a remarkable example of great production design – the famous, famous design. But, nevertheless,* Intolerance *is really Griffith's film, whereas the Bond films are in a profound sense your films, your vision. I think we think about films in terms of memorable energy, memorable moments that fix themselves in our mind. And when we think of Bond films, we think of your images; we think of the kind of scenes, the kind of settings and the kind of action within those settings which are instantly recognisable as yours. This is the very curious thing. In a lot of your work, you became the real author of the films. Is that making too strong a claim?*

Well, I think it's too strong a claim, but also, the Bond films are really a complete chapter on their own. Because, in terms of what we said previously about script, the first one didn't excite me very much, but I could see certain possibilities of expressing myself in a more contemporary way, as a designer, slightly ahead of the time, and slightly tongue-in-cheek. *Dr No* certainly gave me that opportunity, and I also had a very good relationship with Terence Young, who I'd never worked with but who had admired some of my previous films like *The Trials of Oscar Wilde*, and so on. So when we discussed concepts for the film (because it was a low-budget picture, we didn't have time, we were in Jamaica), he said, 'Ken, I will just draw you a plan where I think entrances and the tables, and so on; the geography, the concept I'll leave entirely to you.' So I had really, for the first time I think, carte blanche on that level, and when I came back to England I started scribbling out the designs, and I didn't have anybody looking over my shoulder.

And I had great support, from the Pinewood construction staff of every department – at the time I was prejudiced against Pinewood for various reasons and they simply came up to see me and said, 'Ken, don't worry, anything you will dream up we will help you to achieve, we will come up with new materials, new methods, and so on.' Because by this time I felt we were still using the old methods of building sets and, as a result of that, the look of sets was old, and now there was a sort of explosion, which I don't think would have happened if I hadn't had the support of the art department and the construction department. So in a way that set a style for the film and, when Terence, with Harry Saltzman and Cubby Broccoli arrived back from location, the sets were standing – or three stages were full of sets – and I was somewhat concerned as to how they would react, but Terence just flipped, you know, he said, 'Great', and so on, and then Cubby and Harry followed suit. And so that started the visual concept for the Bond pictures and everybody rose to the tongue-in-cheek approach. So when I've been asked in interviews before about this and I said, 'Well, it became like a democratic debating society', it was perfectly true because from the prop man to the producer, everybody could give ideas. And though I came up with imaginary designs and very often, as Bonds relied less and less on the script (also because we didn't have the original Fleming books any longer), the producer seemed to rely more and more on the look of the picture – whether that was expressed in settings or trying to find exotic locations or gadgets, which really only started with *Goldfinger*. So they really were films on their own. And I had to really surpass myself from film to film. It sometimes happened that we didn't have a cast-iron screenplay and I came up with an important visual idea and, in those cases, the director and the writer used to write the action around certain settings.

66

The extraordinary thing is, when we watch these films, they're completely preposterous; as you say, they are tongue-in-cheek, they send themselves up as they go. Their pure visual excitement is so extraordinary that we are on the edge of our seat as if it mattered. These films, which are totally ridiculous, nobody takes seriously, and yet as you watch them you take them very seriously indeed. But what you are taking seriously is the pure visual excitement: the excitement of the designs becomes, as it were, the dramatic excitement of the films.

Yes, but – you are very complimentary when you say that – but at the same time, you see, somebody like Sean playing Bond was a catalyst for that. If you just had seen interesting visual designs without the character of Bond – which was also a new phenomenon of the Sixties, and so on – you may not have had the same reaction. I think the character of Bond must not be underestimated, you see. Because I understood, more or less, in those days, Bond had to be opposed by a really important villain; an important villain who was conquering, intended to conquer, the whole world and space even. So it was interesting to create these megalomaniacs and provide them with settings which, hopefully, one hadn't seen before, and so on, but the whole chemistry had to work together. They were quite different to any other films I've done.

Oh yes, well, there's a point here, which I'm going to come to. And that is Ipcress. But I was just going to say first, that I remember reviewing one of the early Bond films, and saying Sean Connery is hopelessly miscast as Bond, because he has brown eyes. Bond can't be brown-eyed. Bond, Ian Fleming's Bond, is a blue-eyed character, so Sean Connery is not Bond – but he became Bond. But you see, the other day I watched The Ipcress File. *Now, Sean Connery is a remarkable actor, but Michael Caine is a more remarkable screen presence to my mind, and the whole character of Harry Palmer in* The Ipcress File [**KA**: That's right, yes] – *which was made as a counter, as a riposte to the Bond film – is superior. Both in terms of the star and the dramatic interest,* The Ipcress File *is distinctly superior.*

Well, you see, *The Ipcress File* was an enormous challenge. It was written, as you know, by Len Deighton, and it was one of the early films of Michael Caine, and produced by Harry Saltzman, and Sidney Furie directed it. And we all ganged up in a way against Harry, because Harry thought he was going to make a cheap Bond, whereas we all intended, were very convinced about it, to make almost a counter-Bond – I can't call it an anti-Bond, but you know what I mean. So we ganged up on Harry and every time he came back from Hollywood and came up with these ideas, we wouldn't accept them.

I can give you an example. The film was shot almost entirely on location, so the only studio set was a cell in which Michael Caine is brainwashed. And I had found a house in Grosvenor Place: an Edwardian house which was, I thought, absolutely suitable for the headquarters of the head of MI6 or MI5 – a very large room with three very tall windows, and it was a nice proportion and so on. And Harry said, 'Ken, anything you want' – and that was the office of the chief of MI5, MI6 – 'anything you want from me in terms of computers, and special communications, and so on, I've got it all, just say the word', and so on.

I didn't react to that; in fact, I spent more or less a sleepless night before we were going to start shooting the next morning, and during the night I decided wouldn't it be much more interesting if this military man, played by Nigel Green, would have nothing except a trestle table, with this chair, a camp bed, so the audience immediately knows that he sleeps there at night-time too on several occasions, and not even a chair for anybody else to sit on. And then I decided maybe he would have a bust of some military genius, of Caesar, or Napoleon, or the Duke of Wellington. And so the next morning I said to Sid Furie, 'You know, I've had an idea about this', and I explained this idea to him and he said, 'Give me five minutes, I think it's good. Give me five minutes to think about it.' And he walked off the set and came back after five minutes and said, 'Ken, you're absolutely right. Brilliant idea, that's the way they're going to do it.'

So we start filming and, about an hour later, Harry Saltzman arrives on the set and he is white. And, you know, Harry was very explosive, could be very explosive. Well, he screamed the place down. He told me that I was trying to interfere, that I was trying to make a wedge between him and the director and this is terrible and he's not going to accept it, and he stomped out of the office, as always happens; I mean, film people love a big row. And although everybody had disappeared, his voice could be heard all over the set. I didn't take him too seriously because I'd seen him explode before, and I'd worked with people who are very explosive and somehow I always saw the sense of humour of the thing. And then Sid said, 'Don't worry about Harry, we're going ahead.' And then, about two and a half or three hours later, Harry came back completely calm and he said, 'Well, you may have something.'

You know, what happens on some films is that the chemistry seems to work, which was the case on *The Ipcress File*. We all were excited by the project and by this young actor, Michael Caine, who was completely natural, without any airs and so on, and this cockney character appealed to all of us, so we had a very good creative team on the film. And everybody was involved; I mean, starting with Sid Furie, Michael, we had a wonderful old cameraman called Otto Heller, who started his career by working a hand-cranked camera and, you know, he was an instant cameraman, he never used the light meter, but he was a great artist. So we were really an exciting team and because we were all full of enthusiasm and excitement, I think it reflected on the whole film. And it was the first, almost entire location picture I had done, and it might amuse you, when the film came out, it had a lot of critical acclaim and eventually I was – in what was then the British Film Academy, it was later called BAFTA – nominated for *The Ipcress File* and for *Goldfinger*, which I also had done more or less at the same time. So I had two nominations, and I won for *The Ipcress File*, and Cubby practically wouldn't talk to me afterwards, although it had nothing to do with me; it also appealed to the jury of the Academy in those days.

Yes. I was about to say that, if one could disagree with the claim that you were the British film industry's biggest asset in the second half of the twentieth century, I would offer one possible rival, and that is Michael Caine, but I'm interested in what you said just now, about the chemistry that was engendered by his presence. And also – having the film fresh in my mind – I see the extraordinary quality of Heller's work, it was remarkable.

Yes, he was a true artist. You know, he learnt photography through very primitive means, newsreel, and came over from Germany as a refugee. He became a great friend of mine. I worked with him on a picture as Oliver Messel's assistant, called *The Queen of Spades*, which was a black-and-white film and I admired Otto's work on that. Thorold Dickinson directed it with Edith Evans and Anton Walbrook, and it was a very good-looking picture. It was fascinating to work with Messel. In those first few years when I started in films, I was very lucky to work with people like Messel and, for instance, George Wakhevich, who was a famous Russian opera designer . . .

Who was used by Peter Brook for the immensely famous production of Boris Godunov . . .

Absolutely, and we worked together on a project with Anatol de Brunevald, which was called *World Première*, and we were working at Teddington Studios, it was with Marlene Dietrich, and I think Louise Rainer. And I worked for about three months with George, and he taught me enormously. He did these unbelievable things, very artistic paintings, but then said we would have to build a model of what was Hell – a set, you know, of Dante's Inferno – and I had no idea how to approach it because his designs were so loose. And he said, 'Well, we'll do it in plaster.' He was a great craftsman himself, and he taught me to work with plaster, although this film was never made. I don't know why, but certainly we only worked for three months and then the picture was cancelled.

So I was very fortunate in that way, at the beginning, to have some very good people around. Again, when I worked on *Around the World in Eighty Days* with Cameron Menzies, and then at MGM in England, where the supervising art director was Alfred Junger, who had come from Germany. He was the highest-paid production designer in those days, and somehow he enlightened me and helped me and encouraged me, so it was a very interesting time, in the British film industry. I was relatively young and I never felt, which I later felt, that there was envy: on the contrary, people pushed me and John Bryan, who was a wonderful production designer, encouraged me; Teddy Carrick, who was the supervising art director at Pinewood, spent evenings with me discussing things, and so on. It was quite a different atmosphere than later. Later there was always a certain amount of envy and resentment, the more successful you became. And it's interesting, when I started in films in this country, the art directors, or a large percentage of the art directors at that time, were all cultured, qualified people, they'd been either at the RIBA or had degrees. It was very interesting to, you know, learn from these people, and then, later on, another generation took over, and those were really the generation more of craftsmen: if you discussed painters or styles of antique furniture and so on, they were not as educated as the people I started off with. Now I think it's changed again; I've lost touch with it lately, but I think particularly through television a lot of new talent has come into the business again, people who have an important artistic education – I think it is very important for designers to have that culture in order to really express themselves.

Well, of course, at around this time, developments of what one might do, what one does do, and what happens through the interplay of certain personalities with certain people changed enormously because you got involved in a whole series of Bond films, but that might never have happened. Just remind me of the story, of the interaction between Dr Strangelove *and* Dr No.

Well, if we talk about interaction, I'm not quite sure about that.

I just mean in straight career terms: how did it go, what was happening?

Well, Kubrick, who I admired but didn't know, rang me one day when he arrived in London from New York; he was staying in the Westbury hotel and asked me if I would come to talk to him about this next project, *Dr Strangelove*. He said he had seen *Dr No*, and he liked my work on it and felt I would be the right person to design his next film, which was *Strangelove*. So I met him at the Westbury and we somehow immediately hit it off, you know, there was a chemistry that was working. I was a little fooled by him initially, because he had a lot of charm, but he was also very naïve in some of the questions he asked me, and so on, or at least I thought they were naïve questions, but later on I found this was his way of trying to find out about people. It was something I only found in one other person, and I told him so and I told her so, and that's Barbra Streisand: she had the same sort of intelligence, the same sort of naïvety, which I think is the result of being New York Jewish, and also some of the insecurity feeling – you know, both highly intelligent people, but they want to know everything, there's an enormous curiosity.
So I thought: I've heard about Stanley Kubrick, a difficult director, and

so on. And I said this didn't seem to be the case at all. And as we met again and developed our friendship, our relationship, I sensed that enormous power and incredible brain that he had, and the apparent naïvety is really a very questioning mind. He wants to know what makes you tick and so on. Eventually, of course, this can become counter-productive because, as an artist, or as a designer, I work very instinctively once I've digested the script and the ideas of the director, and so on, but with Stanley I found you had to intellectually justify almost every line, or every design, which was a new experience for me and not an easy experience. But I was very encouraged when – as we are sitting here now – we were sitting, I think, at the Westbury and I started scribbling as we were talking and as he was telling me I would visualise certain things. He liked my scribbles, and again there was almost this childlike enthusiasm and he said, 'Well, I think this is great', and I said, 'My God, this is easy'; you know, little did I know [DS: *laughs*]. I'm convinced that he really did like those first scribbles, but eventually it was a sort of war-room, more Bondian, on two levels.

Then at a later stage, when we had spent two or three weeks together, he said one morning as we were driving to the studio, 'Ken, I think we will have to start rethinking again because I don't know what to do with the second level; you know, we've got to have at least sixty or a hundred extras and they're going to sit up there, and how am I going to use them? So try and come up with a new concept on one level only.' And that really screwed me up, because I'd already started working with the art department. But at the same time, though it was a daily challenge in one way or another, it was a fascinating experience. He always used to say, 'I feel as a director I have the right to change my mind until the cameras are turning', but then eventually of course he changed his mind *after* the cameras started turning, and I had to come up with the solution.

I think one of the greatest advantages of this very close relationship was that I spent every day, about two hours, an hour and a half, driving him to and from Shepperton Studios and we got to know each other pretty well during these trips. Even though part of these trips I had to keep him entertained because he was fascinated by my war experience [DS: *As a pilot*], as a pilot. He wanted to be a pilot of course, as a young man, had an unfortunate near-accident on his first solo flight, so I had to keep him entertained and eventually I had to invent stories [DS: *laughs*]. At the same time we formed a very close relationship and I was probably the first to hear about any of his changes of concept, of changes of mind. You know the story, when Peter Sellers didn't come up with a performance as bomber captain of the B52, and then overnight, with the shoot in two or three days, he sprained his ankle or something, and Stanley felt that this was a good moment to recast and rethink that whole moment, and he came up with a brilliant idea of Slim Pickens as Texan cowboy playing Major T. J. Kong. This changed the whole sequence because he had him riding, as you remember, a nuclear missile into the Russian complex like a cowboy. But it created all sorts of problems for me – but I had to resolve those problems.

Fortunately I had a very good team of people and in particular a wonderful special-effects man, Wally Veevers, who I'd used for many other pictures before and who always, when I came up with a problem that I couldn't solve, said, 'Give me a little time, let me sleep on it and tomorrow morning I'll come up with a solution.' And he did this on *Strangelove* and Stanley of course was impressed; and he did, I suppose, 85 per cent of the effects on *2001*, and if you look at *2001* now, I don't think it is particularly dated. Wally did all those effects without any computers or computer-generated images. He did it with bits of wire and worm gears. But, I mean, as to Kubrick, we would really need a day just to talk about him.

Indeed; well, I worked with Kubrick on one film, on Lolita, *and we used to have lunch every day together, with him and the producer, Jimmy Harris, and the changes in the discussion about the plot, the number of changes of mind – last-minute radical changes of mind – were absolutely astonishing. For people working with him, they were very disturbing and difficult, but on he would go. Do you think possibly, sometimes, he made the wrong judgement in the end?*

No, not on *Strangelove*, I didn't feel that. Later on, with *Barry Lyndon*, he created lots of problems, but on *Strangelove* I didn't feel he made wrong judgements. He also had a wonderful, sort of quirky, humorous writer, Terry Southern, and so every day they created new ideas and new scenes and we all were very much in the spirit of this. He also taught me a lot of things in terms of photography, but the thing that I found fascinating about Stanley is that he would *never* take no for an answer. And this is not just a cliché: when the cameraman said to him this couldn't be done, and Stanley said why?, and he explained, Stanley said, 'Well, it can be done, because if you can't do it I will.' And I was present at numerous occasions when an old technician, who's arrived and knows his job, particularly with a young, new director, would say, 'Well, I'm sorry this isn't possible, Ken', and Stanley always said, 'It can be done.' And later on I adopted this, saying, when I was told it can't be done, that it could be done, you know – and I think this is a very important aspect in the making of films. Having said that, Stanley, maybe with the exception of design, literally could do all the other functions, whether he was editing, whether it was photography, whether it was sound, he knew it all.

You've evoked the excitement of working with Stanley and being with Stanley. Strangelove *was obviously a masterpiece and everybody knew it, and I think that even at that time, if people said, 'What was the greatest set in the history of the cinema?', it was your set for the war-room. Indeed, Steven Spielberg has gone on record as saying that he believes that. So, you had this fantastic excitement, this fantastic success, but when he asked you to work with him on his next project, you refused.*

That's correct, yes. Well, you know it was a very strenuous and trying experience, however much I enjoyed it and learnt an enormous amount, but I felt life was too short really, to be exposed to this brilliant mind for sixteen hours a day. The funny thing is I've got a lot of letters from him when I turned him down on *2001*, which are very amusing, but I can't really quote them now, because I have so much in my head. But on *2001*, when I visited him in New York, I found that he had done one year's research surrounded by experts from NASA and he really knew as much as NASA and the writer Arthur C. Clarke about the subject, and I knew nothing or very little. I felt I could only deal with Stanley and express myself in my way if I could argue on the same level with him about space exploration, and I told him, 'Stanley, you know so much more about this than I, and it's going to inhibit me.' So I turned him down, because I thought the only way I could ever do another picture with Stanley was if I was at least as knowledgeable on the subject matter and the period as he was, because then we could argue on an equal footing.

*But because of that refusal, you were now free to work on a whole series of
Bond films?*

Yes, I worked on Bond films, but interspersed with other films.

*But you certainly wouldn't have made those Bond films if you'd worked on
2001?*

No, that's true. But, David, try to remember, I rarely did one Bond film
after the other: there were always other films in between, which I thought
was important for me because I wanted to do films where the script was
the backbone of the film, the story. The discipline of working on those
types of pictures also appealed to me and then, when I needed therapy to
let myself go, I worked on a Bond film again.

But you knew that if you worked on Strangelove, *you were working on a
film of a very serious kind. Whereas you knew that when you worked on the
Bond films, you were making kitsch.*

Kitsch fantasy, yes. But *Strangelove*, also remember, was during the Cuban
missile crisis and we were all very much aware of the possibilities of atomic
war between the United States and the Soviet Union, and Stanley was
quite paranoid about it. I remember him coming in the evening to the
house in Montpelier Street and poring over maps; he had done these
calculations of nuclear fallout and so on, and advised us to close our bank
accounts and get all our cash out of the bank and, then one day, decided
that the safest place would be Cork in the Republic of Ireland [**DS**: *laughs*],
for nuclear fallout. How he arrived at that decision to this day I don't
know – we thought of some island in the southern Pacific, or Australia, or
New Zealand. No, it was Cork in the Republic of Ireland.

Now, of course there was the tremendous interaction, because the war-room in
Strangelove *and Fort Knox in* Goldfinger *are very much the same vision . . .*

I don't see it that way, I mean if you talk about vision, because *Strangelove*
was an imaginary war-room and my idea was to design something
claustrophobic, enormous, which would help the drama of this whole

sequence. And I had obviously done research into some of these American control bases, which were basically dull, you know, and so on; and they had display maps and so on, like you'd find in a control centre – and I wanted to create these enormous displays, and with this very, very shiny floor: it's a very simple design really. It's composed of these enormous maps which are inclined into the set; a very shiny black floor, in which all these maps are reflected; a thirty-foot- – or whatever – diameter circular table with a thirty-foot hanging light fitment above it. This then inspired Stanley to light all the actors sitting round that table from that light fitting, so we spent hours, you know, like we're sitting here in your kitchen, experimenting – and again he came up with the idea of covering the table in felt so it would accentuate the idea of the President and the generals playing like a game of poker over the future of our world.

So in that sense, it had something to do with Fort Knox, because again Fort Knox was a complete figment of my imagination: I felt if the audiences are admitted to the largest gold depository in the world, into which even the President of the US is not allowed to go, they want to see gold – and as you know, gold is so heavy that it is normally never stacked more than two or three foot high, so I decided to go completely the opposite and stack gold forty foot high and create like a prison of bars with the gold behind them, and the audience seeing all this mountain of gold behind that enormous grille. So in that sense of creating something which is not reality, but which I think was appropriate for the dramatic value of the scene, there was a similarity.

The extraordinary thing is this: everybody thought that Fort Knox in this film was what Fort Knox was like. By the same token, everybody thought there was a war-room at the Pentagon, which was like yours, and everybody knows the story of how when Reagan became President he asked to be shown the war-room. The whole world felt that you'd seen Fort Knox and the Pentagon war-room, which were in fact entirely your own inventions. So you, Ken Adam, invented these secret places. But what they had in common, it seems to me, was this use of these tremendous diagonals whizzing across the scene, of these steep perspectives, which reminds one of Piranesi prisons, in Strangelove *and in the war-room and in the later Bond films. These were your creation, your vision. And the interesting thing is both* Strangelove *and* Goldfinger *were forms of SF . . .*

Science fiction?

Yes. But it is extraordinary how you managed to impose your vision on these totally different stories, these totally different kinds of film, and make them yours.

Yes, well, I felt, you see, that is part of the designer's function, to create his sort of reality and also for the audience to accept it – so it can't be too much science fiction, you know. The audience have to believe that it is possible, because with science fiction they know very often that it is science fiction.

What I think may have influenced me is going back to some of the early films designed in Hollywood and the Cedric Gibbons style of sets, which were not reality: they were beautiful Art Deco nightclubs or apartments with women dressed extremely, in the latest fashions, or in invented fashions, with men in tails, and so on, and the audiences did accept them, in what was a pure form of escapism from reality that they saw every day. And so, I felt that in both the pictures you are talking about, I hopefully could create a form of escapism for the audience, because they didn't know what the war-room was like, they didn't know what Fort Knox looked like: I certainly didn't know what Fort Knox looked like, but I knew it was probably very dull. Film is also a form of entertainment and I think one must never forget that. In films, if you have the opportunity to make the audience dream or escape from everyday reality, then you are halfway to success.

But what do you mean: halfway to success? What is success?

Success of the dramatic impact of the scene or a series of scenes played in that ambience.

But the thing is, that in the case of your kitsch Bond films, one's watching, yes, but nobody takes it seriously . . .

But when you were talking about Fort Knox, they did take it seriously [**DS**: *Yes*], because United Artists received hundreds of letters after the film came out asking, 'How was it that Ken Adams was allowed to go inside Fort Knox?'

Yes, but they didn't take the content of the film seriously. [**KA**: No, obviously not.] *On the other hand, maybe I'm being wise after the event and not seeing the way that we saw* Strangelove *at the time. It was a great work of social satire, of political satire* [**KA**: Absolutely], *it brought us face-to-face with reality and although obviously it was an incredibly crazy creation, nevertheless, when we watched that film we felt very frightened for the future of the world. And the wild and crazy character played by George Scott – General 'Buck' Turgidson – the extravagance of it was extraordinary, but nevertheless we felt all the sinister implications of American military power, and people who had it. But you managed to function, both in the purely frivolous, the realm of the guy in the metal bowler hat, throwing it through space, and on the other hand in the action of* Strangelove, *which is profoundly serious.*

Yes, you are absolutely right in your analysis, and obviously I was very much aware of the serious aspect of *Dr Strangelove*, but I still felt that by creating the war-room set, I could create a framework in this underground bomb shelter which was not departing from what the audience might accept as reality. I felt it was absolutely right, and I think Stanley felt that way, in terms of what he was trying to say, and it helped him to go into this hellz-a-poppin' aspect of making the film, which was probably the best way of trying to influence world audiences about this terrible possibility of nuclear disaster.

I see a picture emerging here: if you worked with Stanley the tension was tremendous, the nervous tension was something you couldn't face all the time. When you were working on Bond films you knew what you were doing, you had certain formulae which you could develop, which you could do in more complex and sophisticated ways, and you were master, you were circus master in your own circus. It was possible for you to handle it because you were in charge and therefore it didn't make the same terrible demands as working with a personality as strong as yourself. Nevertheless, you agreed to work with Stanley again, on Barry Lyndon, *and you said that on that film you thought that Stanley did make mistaken judgements.*

Absolutely, yes. And you know, I didn't really want to do *Barry Lyndon*. I was working on a picture in the South of France, called *The Last of*

Sheila, but Stanley when he wants you, he always finds you. It's actually quite an amusing story: he said right at the beginning of the whole conversation that he was not going to pay me the usual money and it was not a lot, you know, so I said: 'Well, Stanley, that's fine', you know, 'because I'm not going down on my fee.' And so he said, 'Well, Ken, it means I'll have to use the second-best production designer', and I said, you know, 'Stanley, I'm not mad at you, be my guest', and that was it! And five weeks later a completely different Stanley contacted me and said – it was a shy, naïve Stanley who said, 'Gee, Ken, I'm afraid that the second-best production designer doesn't seem to understand what I want and your money is no problem, so please work on this film with me, and I think we can have a lot of fun.' And that's how I accepted – even though I had been quite relieved after the first phone conversations, I remember going back to my wife Letizia and saying I'd got out of this one! And so, we started on *Barry Lyndon*, and it's a very complicated story, but I'll try to keep it simple.

I think, first of all, Stanley felt that Thackeray was as good as the majority of scriptwriters at that time, because he said to us, 'I think he wrote this like a film script and so I'm going to film the *Barry Lyndon* of Thackeray as he wrote it.' I was with him at the time and I said to him, 'Stanley, I agree you may be absolutely right about the quality of a lot of scriptwriters, but I still think it has to be a moving picture and at the time of Thackeray this didn't exist', and he said, 'Well, I will deal with this.' Of course, with his feeling of secrecy, he would never issue a whole script, but simply have pages out of Thackeray Xeroxed and then presented to people who had to start working on the film, and eventually he got into trouble, he was working all through the night sometimes, writing scenes and creating scenes.

The other problem, a much bigger one for me, was that I could not get him out of his house to look at locations. At that time he was living in Borehamwood and I think the reason why he was so reluctant to go on location was that he had just received a lot of threatening letters as a result of *Clockwork Orange*. And he was really quite worried about his life, the life of his family, and so on, and he felt safe in the surroundings of his home. So he created like a war-room, miniature war-room in his garage, with Ordnance Survey maps put on the wall, little flags, and so on, from a five-mile radius around Borehamwood to I think it was a twenty-mile radius, and he employed young photographers – they weren't really photographers; they were kids, including my niece, Nicky, who was eighteen, who knew how to take pictures on a Nikon camera or whatever. They were sent round every day in ever-increasing radiuses around his home to see if they could find interesting locations, and so on, which was, of course, a completely impractical way of working, because I had all the Pevsner books and knew most of the important homes in that vicinity. But I think Stanley's motivation was another one: (a) he didn't want to go out of the house, but also (b) we had a slide-screening every evening of the photographs these kids had taken, and he insisted on every one of these young boys or girls taking a tripod with them, because he wanted every photograph in natural light, and he said even if it's dark, even if you've only got a dim light, you still can get an exposure. And in the evening, the voyeur came out in Stanley, because he was fascinated sometimes when some of the interiors had been shot and a bed was unmade or something – and I think, quite frankly speaking, a good director has to be a voyeur as well.

But did you find the locations?

No, we didn't find the locations, and Stanley's theory – which was that you never know what's around the corner – is probably partly true, but not if you are trying to do a period picture and not if those kids don't know what they are photographing. So I was almost a school teacher at those screenings, because – also it was very funny – what appealed to Stanley was really Victoriana rather than the eighteenth century, you see, and I got into terrible arguments with him, you know, and I said, 'Stanley, you can't use that, that's typical Victorian wallpaper', and he said, 'What?' and I said, 'Stanley, I know it is'; he said, 'Prove it.' The one thing I will say is, it gave Stanley plenty of time to acquaint himself with the eighteenth century, because we had every textbook on the eighteenth century, we used to go by Pevsner or 'the Pevsner tips', we used to call it, to find interesting houses. Finally – I think it must have been after five months – I got him to go out on location for the first time, and I will never forget it: he turned round to me and he said, 'Gee, Ken, those kids didn't know where to point their camera.' And I said, 'Well, how did you expect them to? They didn't have a script and, you know, there's a certain limit to what you find in the twenty-mile radius outside Elstree or Borehamwood.' So, that was very, very frustrating.

Also, the main concept he had, partly from his sense of economy and partly because he felt more at home with real locations, was to shoot the entire picture on location. I had enormous arguments with him because I always felt: Yes, by all means use fabulous-looking buildings, interiors, exteriors, on location, but very often I, in the studio, can create more of what you are looking for, because even the artists of that period, when you look at Hogarth or Rowlandson, satirised the period, and so on. And Stanley was very much attracted by that, and I said, you know, 'It's easier in many cases for me to do that in the studio than to go to some incredible stately home where they don't allow you to move their paintings or furniture, and at the same time charge you a great deal of money.' And on that level I was proved right, because once all the stately homes found we were looking for locations, the money ran out and we had to pay a fortune: even Lady Lyndon's house finally became, I think, six stately homes over Britain, which we filmed [**DS**: *laughs*].

But he felt it was the only way he could achieve that documentary aspect of the eighteenth century and obviously the end result was fabulous from a visual point of view, but very costly. Not only in terms of money but, of course, costly in terms of my health, because as you know I eventually had a breakdown because I had to fight him on almost every level. To get him to Ireland was a major achievement – part of the film takes place in Ireland – and then to find the locations was hard, as Cromwell had destroyed so many earlier buildings and I was tearing all over Ireland, trying to find what I'd think was right. And then he wanted to shoot the continental locations there as well, which was an additional challenge. So it became very frustrating and that's to put it mildly, because he was a very possessive person, I think we had like a love–hate relationship, it was almost like a marriage: he insisted on me seeing daily rushes after the unit had seen them, which was at eleven o'clock at night, and then collect him at five o'clock in the morning, so I didn't get any sleep – he didn't get any sleep either – and eventually my resistance just evaporated.

I mean, one day he said to me, 'Where are we shooting tomorrow?' and I said, 'I don't know' and he said, 'But you did some great shots in the mountains' and I said, 'Yes', and he said, 'Well, why can't you go there tomorrow?', so I said, 'But you know, that was taken on a mountain track?'

At the time we were working like a mobile column, where each department has its own van or minibus, and I remember saying, 'This convoy of sixty vehicles, if you meet any other vehicle up there or something and just turn around at the top, it's going to be a major disaster.' He said, 'Who gives a shit, let's do it in the morning.' And we did that. And of course whatever I had prophesied happened, it was a complete shambles, and we lost two-thirds of a day, but on our way down, after this awful way of turning everybody around, suddenly there was a break in the cloud and we had the most incredible sky; and we stopped the whole convoy, we got the horse out, and Hardy Kruger out, put him on the horse and shot him, and it looked like a Goya painting, and so it worked, you know.

But by this time I felt I took all of Stanley's problems on my shoulder, and suddenly I was apologising for the fiasco, which was nothing to do with me, which was entirely Stanley's responsibility. I was pretty far gone by this stage, and Letizia said to Stanley, 'Ken can't carry on this way.' So at this moment he realised that I wasn't well and he said, 'Well, get the best medical treatment for this, don't do this, don't do that, and I will do everything you have asked me to do.' And he then became, obviously, very concerned and also very caring about me, but it's quite a strange story because I was really seriously ill and the psychiatrist looking after me finally decided that the only way he could get me well again was to cut this umbilical cord between me and Stanley. And Stanley of course was very scared, but, you know, he was so wrong because when I finally got home . . .

You finally got . . .

Back to the house in London, he had been kept informed of the various locations I'd chosen, and he was keeping exactly to it. And he rang me up the moment I arrived from the clinic and said, 'Ken, I just wanted you to know that I'm going to send a second unit to Potsdam to do all the shots you asked for and I would like you to direct the shots', and that created such a conflict within me that within twenty-four hours I was back in the clinic.

(Laughs) And for that you got an Academy Award?

And for that I got an Academy Award, yes.

BRIDGET RILEY 1967

Recorded in 1967, and later included in *The Mind's Eye: Bridget Riley, Collected Writings 1965–1999*, edited by Robert Kudielka, 2000.

DAVID SYLVESTER *You're very conscious, of course, of the optical effects you want to present?*

BRIDGET RILEY Yes, but not entirely conscious. Though I can foresee certain things happening, it's such an enormous field that things will always happen that you don't anticipate.

How often do you get optical effects which you completely failed to anticipate and that you want to suppress?

Quite often. Sometimes I can control them. Sometimes I can suppress them without damaging the rest. But, for instance, in the painting called *Breathe*, those echoes that run up from the base and shatter the forms right up to the top – though they are necessary in three-quarters of the painting, I don't want them at the top. But I cannot get rid of them at the top without eliminating them from the whole canvas altogether. They are a flaw, one that I have to accept.

What of Deny? *It seems to me that two optical effects happen there. One is that the little ovals, when seen from a certain distance, seem like pieces of reflecting steel, cut out and stuck to the painting, shiny and light-catching. Was that part of the intention?*

No, it wasn't.

Secondly, there's a curious effect, when you stand close to the painting, of a thick grey mist or smoke between you and the painting. Was that part of the intention?

Yes . . . obscuring, negating it.

83

What else was in your intention?

To oppose a structural movement with a tonal movement, to release increased colour through reducing the tonal contrast. In the colour relationship of the darkest oval with the ground, the change of colour is far more pronounced than it is between the lightest oval and the ground, where you get a tonal contrast – almost a black-and-white relationship – happening instead, which knocks the colour down.

Do you sometimes find that in the end an optical effect which was not one that you anticipated in a painting turns out to be the one that interests you most?

Sometimes. And sometimes I'll examine that one separately, more fully in another situation.

You paint from drawings, and you usually make a number of drawings for every painting, and a great many drawings which don't lead directly to a painting. Are these ever drawings made for the sake of making drawings, or are all your drawings made with the idea of doing a painting?

They're always towards a painting. When I've selected a unit which I'm thinking of using in a painting, I make this unit visible, so that I can see its attendant problems and its potential.

When the unit first comes into your mind do you already have an idea of what sort of scale the painting is going to be?

No. The scale comes from the physical thing, from the visual statement.

During the making of the drawings?

Yes.

How often have you done a painting in one scale and found that it was wrong and that you had to begin again?

Very seldom.

When you're wrong, do you do the discarded painting again on a different scale? Or do you tend to be bored with the idea once you've got the scale wrong the first time?

No, I do it again.

But you are saying that before you've done a drawing you've got very little idea whether the final thing is going to be big or small?

Yes, that's true.

But you nowadays habitually paint larger than before. Would you like to redo your old paintings larger?

No. They are right as they are.

Meaning that the ideas in your early paintings were ideas for paintings on a smaller scale, necessarily?

Necessarily.

And that now your ideas are for paintings on a larger scale?

Yes.

Does the fact that you are working on a larger scale give a feedback to the ideas themselves, so that these are now mostly ideas for larger paintings, or is it that, among the ideas which you make drawings of, you then carry through those which demand a larger scale and tend not to bother with those which would be done on a smaller scale?

No, it's the first one. Paintings breed. You work in certain groups. I remember before my first American show I started to work on a group of things which all became small paintings. There was nothing I could do to change the scale. The ideas demanded small canvases.

85

Do you want your work to be aggressive towards the spectator? Do you like it to hurt your eyes?

I don't mind either way. But I remember being very surprised when people first complained that it hurt their eyes, because it has never hurt mine.

No?

No, never. Not *hurt* them.

Does it make them water?

No.

Doesn't it give you a pain?

No – no *pain*! It gives me pleasure.

Does it give you that famous admixture, pleasure–pain?

Possibly, in that it is a stimulating, an active, a vibrating pleasure.

Comparable to what?

Running . . . early morning . . . cold water . . . fresh things, slightly astringent . . . things like this . . . certain acid sorts of smells.

Really? You enjoy certain acid sorts of smells?

Yes. I don't like heavy smells. I like light, buoyant smells.

Like ammonia?

Oh no! Like wood being cut.

Yes, but what about wood being cut when the saw gives a sound like a squeaky chalk on a blackboard?

I don't mind that. That blackboard sound has never bothered me.

Well, that's very interesting. It may throw light on why you don't worry about the eye-jerking effect of your paintings. Because I think there's no doubt . . .

Don't forget I see them grow. That could make a difference.

I don't think it's that, because it seems you don't mind other things which tend to get most people on a nerve. But the fact that you see the paintings grow – does that make a difference? The painting I have, for example, I've had it for years, but it still hurts my eyes.

Well, only in that I can never see a painting of mine quite as other people do.

Don't they have an optical effect on you, for example?

Of course, certainly they do.

Now, if they have an optical effect, don't they have an eye-hurting effect also?

No, these are different qualities. I don't experience this eye-hurting business, but I experience the optical effect.

You see the lines moving to and fro?

Yes, but I find that an exhilarating thing, a stimulating sensation – never painful physically.

That sounds very masochistic, Bridget.

I have been accused of that, but I don't think it is that.

If other people, while liking your work, find it eye-hurting, what do you feel about that?

I think it is beside the point. I think this would be a very offhand response, simply to react like that.

Well, believe me, it can go on. I've lived with one of your paintings.

Yes, but surely you get involved with the painting? And I don't see how you could get involved with the painting if you only experience this eye-hurting effect.

No, I didn't say I only experience it as that. I think it's rather like certain music by John Cage and La Monte Young, which, while one responds to it aesthetically, is nevertheless undoubtedly painful to hear. And there's no getting round the fact that it is painful to hear and that it really produces a noise level or a pitch level which makes it in some sense disagreeable. I don't think one ever reaches the stage when this ceases to be an element in one's experience of it.

Yes, I see that.

But you've certainly no aggressive intention towards the spectator, have you?

No, not as such.

Do you think of your work as aggressive?

Not necessarily. I think of there being colossal energies involved . . . in the medium . . . in the units, intervals, lines . . . I know that they are high-voltage, potentially.

Does that mean you want the spectator to get something like an electric shock?

I want the spectator to experience the *power* of these elements. For instance, I called one painting *Static* in the sense of a field of static electricity. It is visual prickles. But I don't find that a painful physical thing. It's a quality: as velvet is smooth, so this is a sparkling texture – visually. The key to this, I think, is in the actual stuff I am dealing with –

the elements themselves. This may strike you as a strange comparison, but I feel that when Michelangelo said that he let a figure out of the stone, so I feel that I let the energy out of the forms, the elements, via the relationships.

When do you think of the titles?

Sometimes while making the drawings, rarely while carrying out the painting, sometimes after it's finished.

You say, for example, that Static *is so called because of the idea of a field of static electricity. At what point did that association first come to you?*

At one stage I thought of calling the painting *Discharge*, with the idea of arrows, say, being discharged in your face as you looked at it. I rejected that, but it led me to the other. Actually, I thought of the painting itself when I was going up a mountain in France which had a vast expanse of shale at the top. It was an extremely hot day. I was getting anxious because we were going in a car up a steep narrow road. Visually it was total confusion; I felt there was no possibility of understanding the space of this situation. You couldn't tell whether this shimmering shale was near or far, flat or round. One of us said it was like the desert. We found it so alarming that we got out of the car, which of course intensified the sensation. But it was much cooler at the top, and into my mind came the beginnings of *Static*, a mass of tiny glittering units like a rain of arrows.

Do you often get ideas for paintings from visual experience of reality?

Occasionally, but in a roundabout way, in that visual experience, all experience, of reality adds up to a whole thing, an overall state of being. One might go to a strange city and feel extremely desolate, might have missed people whom one thought one was going to see, might be oppressed by the city. It might be built of dark stone. The houses might be very tall, one might feel cold, and have this feeling of oppression. Those three or four days could add up to a totally oppressive period. These are the sorts of things that I could recognise later in one of my paintings, if I had felt them deeply enough.

MALCOLM MORLEY 1989

This is in two parts. The first is an essay which accompanied the interview recorded in 1989. Both were published in *Malcolm Morley*, the catalogue to an exhibition at the Anthony d'Offay Gallery, London in 1990. The essay bore the title 'A Dance of Paint, A Dance of Death', and the interview 'Showing the View to a Blind Man'.

I

You can turn away from the canvas to look at something else and still be assailed by the paint as if particles of it were being propelled in every direction. Even as its energy seems to fill the room, its surface seems somehow to remain immaculate. Moreover, the image presents vertiginous spaces which behave like vortices, yet the surface still seems flat and solid as a slab of marble. The work is a paradigm of contained violence. It always has been with Morley, but the polarity becomes increasingly assertive.

Morley is very much an international artist, perhaps in rather the same way as de Kooning. Any self-respecting professional observer coming to the work for the first time would expect to be able to tell that it was painted in New York and by a European hand; he would hope to be able to tell that the hand in the one case was Dutch, English in the other. At the same time, Morley's language is peculiarly inclusive. His handling of paint seems full of quotations from or reminders of a wide variety of twentieth-century painterly painters – Pollock, de Kooning, Nolde, Kokoschka, Matisse, early Rouault, mid-20s Soutine (those large red areas in the recent work which seem to be Madeleine Castaing's dress).

The packing-in of masses of figurative detail means that the brushwork often evokes that of past masters: Constable's large oil-sketches come to mind; so, in all his flashiness, does Lawrence. The other day, in the Metropolitan Museum, I was made to think of Morley by Frans Hals's picture of a mardi gras revel. I remembered having long ago compared this work with de Kooning's Women pictures, but that had largely been to prove a point about de Kooning's rootedness in a Dutch tradition; Morley's affinity is more comprehensive. A rearing mass of faces, lewd looks, grimacing mouths, bawdy gestures, diverse genital metaphors, thrusting movement in all directions, white impasto for the lace and the parallel pleats along the arms in a reddish dress, a mood – save in the character at top right, who has everything under control – of Dionysian fever, a Falstaff at the centre of the action, at the periphery an assortment of fleshy faces, ubiquitous ambiguities in the performance and the roles including the likelihood that the girl is a boy, pleasure pursued frantically, chaos come again.

Like the work of, say, Magritte or Jasper Johns, Morley's has been haunted by objects belonging to his boyhood. With Magritte such objects include reading primers, stereoscopic images, paper cut-outs, masks, metal puzzles, printed puzzles, comic strips, adventure books; with Johns, targets, flags, numbers, lettering, rulers, balls, maps; with Morley, tin soldiers, toy weapons, model airplanes, model ships, books about warfare (picture books but also things like the Biggles books) and the Coronation Mug which was handed out to schoolchildren at the time of the crowning of King George VI. Morley was six, and he says that the decoration of this mug has been the source of his idea of colour.

His Rosebud, lost to him when destroyed in an air raid on London, was a painted balsa wood model he made of a famous warship, his favourite among several such models. It has come back, it appears, in one of the sculptures he has lately started making – a grey model of a battle cruiser mounted on a tall grey oval plinth which stands for the ocean and succeeds in evoking its depth and somehow in suggesting its perils. Like most of the eight sculptures Morley has made so far, it strongly relates in its sense of deliquescence and concomitant threat of loss to Medardo Rosso and to Giacometti. These sculptures also relate to Giacometti's, of course, in the ways in which image and base are inseparable.

Giacometti told me that he found tin soldiers in shop windows more relevant to reality than most contemporary figurative sculpture. Morley's sculptures mostly recall toy soldiers or their tanks or guns. They deal, it seems to me, with two sets of feelings experienced in boyhood. There is the feeling of attachment to certain objects which is stronger than any admitted feeling about human beings and which therefore produces acute anxiety or desolation about the fear or reality of their loss. And there is the feeling as puberty comes of the frightening force of one's growing virility together with its antidote, the identification of objects which resemble the irrepressible member in an entertaining way. Morley's two images of machine-gunners are splendidly potent symbols of this sort. The sculptures are reminders that toys are our education in the facts of death and life.

'What is fascinating now,' Francis Bacon said in 1962, 'is that it's going to become much more difficult for the artist, because he must really deepen the game to be any good at all.' Morley is one of the few who seem to be deepening the game, which means, of course, always playing for high stakes. He invests exceptional technical resources in pushing pictorial languages to ridiculous extremes. Above all, his involvement in a pursuit to their limits of the drama and desperation of existence drives him as if without fear to explore the frontiers of madness.

He is not lighthearted in his use of ancient myths. Most modern artists, including Picasso, seem to be using the myths, as, say, Boucher did, as a pretext for making art of a certain sort. Morley seems to be using his art to brood upon the myths. He gives them both weight and immediacy, in a fashion which I find very reminiscent of Max Beckmann. He conveys a feeling that those were titanic days. He seems to have some urgent inner involvement with the stories to inspire the iconography he invents for them, full of new ironic conceits – for example, in that tremendous dance of death, *Black Rainbow over Oedipus at Thebes,* the way the letters in the Greek inscription across the base of the image are spaced so that they look like letters in a card for testing eyesight.

That was done knowingly. Other things done unknowingly are even more relevant to my point. I was looking for the first time at another picture on the same scale painted a year earlier and called *Aegean Crime.* I recognised the characters from other works as being based on sculptures from which Morley had made drawings in various museums, the figure on the left being, he said, a French Romanesque Christ, the head at top right Minoan and the bust at bottom right a Roman copy of a bust of Alexander the Great. After looking at the picture for some time, awed by its atmosphere of tragedy, menace and revenge, I thought about the title and started asking myself what the subject could be. The clue seemed to be in the head at top right, its eyes veiled by a venomous green and therefore perhaps the blinded eyes of another Oedipus image. But there was too much going on that suggested a different interpretation. That dominant figure must be Clytaemnestra with a baleful gaze and the bearded head below her of a man largely submerged in water must be Agamemnon slaughtered in his bath; the Christ-like figure would be a symbol of sacrifice, while the two boats in the picture would represent, first, Agamemnon's fleet becalmed until he offered his daughter up for sacrifice, second, the vessel which brought him back to his bloody end. It was all as obvious and inevitable as the solution to a crossword clue once it is found. When I next saw Morley I congratulated him on his portrayal of Agamemnon and Clytaemnestra. Politely he told me that he could not remember having heard of them. Three cheers for the collective unconscious.

II

Seeing the world grey

Colour is such an emotional thing. One of Piaget's tests on children's perception of colour showed that children whose parents were divorced saw less colour. They literally saw things greyer, and children who came from a happy family literally perceived colour as being brighter. And I remember myself seeing the world grey. I could not see colour in the world for many years as a young painter.

Showing the view to a blind man

I've been writing a film script for ten years. It's the story of Thomas, Thomas the painter. And it's a saga from World War II to the present time, a sort of cultural *War and Peace* with the social history of New York thrown in, with a complete reconstruction of the Cedar Bar.

It has a lovely metaphor on seeing for the modern artist. When I was a little boy my grandmother took me to the seaside at Folkestone and we were walking along the boardwalk and it was the most beautiful day, with sailboats sailing by, billowing white clouds, stuff like that. I must have been about six or seven. And I went up to a man sitting on a bench and tugged at his coat and said, Oh! Look at the ships, look at the ships, aren't they nice! And he said to me, Can you read, sonny? And I said, Yes, I can read. And he said, Can you read what's on this button? And it said, BLIND. And at that moment my grandmother came up and grabbed my hand and said, Can't you see he's blind? I wanted to disappear completely.

And that's a metaphor of myself as an artist, to show the view to a blind man. I have that in the film script. Thomas is in a sailor suit. I've got that indelibly in my mind. The man is wearing black glasses and the reflection of the boats is on his glasses, but he's not able to see them. *Black Rainbow over Oedipus at Thebes* is a metaphor for blindness.

Black Rainbow over Oedipus at Thebes

The Oedipus painting looks like brown shit. I think this brownness is rather disconcerting, but I love the idea which Barney Newman, who was my great teacher really, gave me that in Hebrew the word for Adam and Earth is the same word. That just blew me apart.

The origins of this painting are extraordinary. One is a little drawing that I made in Greece at the theatre at Epidaurus, at a performance of *Oedipus Rex*. A most fantastic experience even without knowing a word of Greek, and I was riveted. For the chorus they have a whole regiment of modern army soldiers, about a thousand, dressed up as ancient Greeks, coming over the hill. And you know that they have been walking over this hill for three thousand years, the same spot, the same rock. Oedipus looks as if he's made of stone, with his eyes gouged out. It's just fantastic. Anyway, I made this drawing and I made a lithograph from it which I used for part of this painting. And I took the rainbow from another watercolour that I made in Africa over Mount Kenya. The three figures below are local people who have a boat here in Bellport.

Then it was very important to me to make the title. The work of putting on the lettering was damned difficult because I had to use stencils. I wanted these letters to float, saying in Greek, Black Rainbow over Oedipus at Thebes. I couldn't tell you why, but I love the sound of it, the way it comes off your mouth. The titles are very important to me. It would be very interesting if you just took all the titles of the paintings and made a poem from them, without anything else.

Beautiful ground stroke, by God!

I only want to paint in oil paint on canvas, not in oil paint on oil paint. I'm not an oil painter on oil paint, I'm an oil painter on canvas. And I must have that ground all the time to paint upon. It feels horrible when I start to paint on top of paint which is still drying underneath at different levels, with skin on top.

I once had this idea of starting a magazine called *Oil Painting*. It wouldn't discuss anything else, and a critic would write in the way a sports writer would write when looking at tennis. He would say, Beautiful ground stroke, by God, look at the way he stroked that, and in that yellow, that Naples yellow!

What oil paint wants

You could make oil paint function in a transparent fashion, but you would have to alter the material of it. Oil paint functions more powerfully, more effectively, if you are using it in terms of its own nature. It does not want to be thinned down. Watercolour wants to be thin. I think that all of the work I do is very involved in what the nature of the material itself is.

Painter and sculptor

The painter looks at the landscape and paints it. Does the sculptor look at the landscape and sculpt it?

Snowstorm in Washington Square

When I was making my ugly pictures, ugly from the idea of doing something for yourself that you've never seen before, I used to throw up at the end of each picture, in front of it. It was so appallingly horrible and it was so appallingly true. It took me seven years to be able to look at them. Now I think they're beautiful. I've got some that are really insane, these paintings, shapes like equilateral triangles, cutting triangles out of the grid and looking at them. I was very involved with Buckminster Fuller's 60-degree thing and going out into nature to paint through these holes. In fact I was once in the Village doing it. It was in a snowstorm and I was painting a snowman in the middle of a snowstorm in Washington

Square. I had this triangular painting with a triangle cut out of it in the middle of the grids, which were triangular. So I'm looking through this triangle and an eye comes through and says, My God, it's Malcolm! And it was Cy Twombly and Rauschenburg and a whole gang of people just wandering around in the snow. It was kind of embarrassing, a guy out in the snow with an equilateral triangle looking like some kind of witch.

Pleasure

Why do I paint? I do it to get pleasure. But I'm not easy to please. So it becomes a sort of carrot.

Bleeding eyes

Cézanne said that he felt his eyes bleeding when he took them off one object to the next. Can you imagine that idea? It's Oedipus again, of the bleeding eyes. You can imagine the idea of the eyes sucking, like a suction pad. I feel like that myself sometimes, that the eye sucks onto this and that it hurts to let go and move on to the next place.

Painting as a heartbeat

I have this theory about smoking and the heartbeat of the mother – that in the womb, maybe, you're hearing the heartbeat and that the impulse towards repetition, for example, masturbation or compulsive smoking, anything repeating itself, is an assurance of that original heartbeat neurotically sustained. It's just the neurosis of repetition in itself, it almost doesn't matter what is being repeated. Artists fall very quickly into the idea of repetition and compulsion as a form of security.

Breathing out is getting lost

Often, when making a painting, there's some kind of resistance, and it changes from picture to picture. In one instance it might be the resistance of the canvas that doesn't feel quite good, that you don't have quite the right ground. Or another is the resistance that you don't have the right balance in the medium. Another resistance is that the brushes aren't quite right, etc., etc. And for years the next picture would be a kind of plan to try to solve the problem of resistance in the last picture. After many years I found out that it didn't matter what you did. I decided that the resistance was just self-consciousness in doing something and that, to use Norman Brown's lovely phrase, the way to true happiness was to get lost.

It works like a pulse, getting lost or not getting lost. Almost to a degree of inhalation and exhalation. Breathing in is being self-conscious and breathing out is getting lost. When I've self-consciously mixed some paint I can go and get lost until I've used up that material. Then I mix it again. So I have spurts of getting lost and of being very aware of myself as a doing creature throughout the paintings as they happen.

I've made friends with my resistance, it's no longer my enemy. I don't battle on through no matter what. I stop and ask what it is. For example, I couldn't paint *Gloria* after a while. Then I realised there was too much to look at and I covered most of the canvas with brown paper and started in a new place. I only had a little white canvas left to look at and I was able then to proceed; I had lowered the resistance. There had been so much input coming from what I had previously painted that it was slowing down the painting of new areas, so I concealed from myself what I had done before. I have to paint in a way like a typist typing a manuscript and not knowing at the end how it reads.

The whole thing in New York

The whole thing in New York when I came here was that you had to do something new that hadn't been done before. But everything you do has been done before one way or another. All those stripes, they're all in Renaissance painting – in little corners. The history of newness in art resides in looking at the left-hand corner of previous painting and blowing that up. You take a de Kooning and blow that up and you get field painting. You could take a detail out of any of these early Renaissance paintings and you've got beautiful modernistic art.

HOWARD HODGKIN 1982

Recorded for the Landseer/Arts Council film, *Howard Hodgkin* (1982). This version was edited in collaboration with the artist, and appeared in the catalogue published by the Whitechapel Gallery in 1984, in connection with the touring exhibition organised by the British Council, *Howard Hodgkin: Forty Paintings, 1973–84*.

DAVID SYLVESTER *A lot of your pictures are painted over a period of three, four, five years, or longer. How do you know a painting is finished?*

HOWARD HODGKIN My pictures are finished when the subject comes back. I start out with the subject and naturally I have to remember first of all what it looked like, but it would also perhaps contain a great deal of feeling and sentiment. All of that has got to be somehow transmuted, transformed or made into a physical object, and when that happens, when that's finally been done, when the last physical marks have been put on and the subject comes back – which, after all, is usually the moment when the painting is at long last a coherent physical object – well, then the picture's finished and there is no question of doing anything more to it. My pictures really finish themselves.

When you speak of the subject's coming back or the picture's being a coherent physical object at long last, you're talking about exceedingly subtle exercises of a sensibility. What is a finished picture, really? For example, take that marvellous Degas portrait of Hélène Rouart which the National Gallery has acquired lately. Now, according to conventional art-historical wisdom, the painting is not quite finished. Do you think it's unfinished?

I think the whole picture is deliberately made to look like an unfinished painting. There are those curious red and blue pastel lines round the arm, along the edge of the body, which are often running almost in tandem side by side, and they actually make it look more incomplete there. They lighten the atmosphere, they lighten the surface, they make a little sort of breaking-up of the surface which makes it more like other parts of the picture which are more loosely painted. Because it had got a bit tight in

99

places in the painting of the body, and clearly Degas was trying to soften it again, those red and blue marks were added to the image to make the illusionism greater. To me, that picture has the most extraordinary sense of reality about it because of the fact that what you see has not been finally made into the sort of tight image of realism that we've been led to expect in all sorts of ways, but has the kind of glancing, slightly dematerialised quality that one does actually see in reality.

And do you want to get that glancing, dematerialised quality?

Yes, I do, I want to get the sort of evasiveness of reality into my pictures. I mean, looking at you now, I don't see Ingres's portrait of Monsieur Bertin, for example. Because I'm always seeing something else and something more. I might be looking past you or looking at the light falling on part of you or thinking of you. So it's my idea of you as well as what I see that's in my mind. But this kind of realism which depends also a lot on illusionism, is, of course, evanescent, frail and difficult to establish. And I think what's extraordinary about that picture of Degas's is that early in his life he was painting very Ingres-inspired pictures, where his idea of someone both from seeing them and knowing them is turned into a sort of iconic, solid, hard representation, and that he went from there into something which is much more like life itself.

He worked on that painting for a long time; so one can get that glancing dematerialised quality when doing that. And then there's de Kooning's Woman *series, which were all reworked again and again and which he said he wanted to be like glimpses. One might suppose naïvely that the way to try and reproduce that evasiveness of reality would be through* alla prima *painting, but Degas and de Kooning weren't content with that and evidently you're not.*

Because *alla prima* painting doesn't in fact contain enough. It only contains as much as you have had time to put down. And the great problem, when one wants to add more, is to work on and on and on till you can not only return to the original nature of the subject – but as a painting, as something else – but also return to the original freshness. And that's taken me years to get even near. Because usually when one goes on working at a painting, there are obviously physical and technical difficulties that make it less and less likely to be fresh at the other end. To be brief and witty at the end of five years' work is obviously a very difficult thing, but can easily contain much more than doing it straight away. And the glancing immaterial quality has got to refer to a great deal. You need to take in an awful lot for it to have meaning. What takes a long time is to give it meaning, to enclose within it emotions, feelings, and obviously a quantity of impressions rather than the single one that one might have been able to include in an *alla prima* beginning. Which is often how I do begin. In fact, the subject-matter of my pictures in sort of literal terms is often established in one sitting, as it were. Like that picture on the wall, which is just blue marks, but is the entire composition which I will go on working on for a very long time.

Going on for a long time is a gamble, of course, a necessary gamble. Even with great artists, it often wrecks pictures, irredeemably. Does it with you?

Almost never.

Why is that?

I think because I only go on with them until they're finished. I've sometimes deliberately shown pictures when they've been unfinished, because I'm uncertain as to how to go on, and it's a great boon, obviously, to be able to see them somewhere else and in the company of other pictures and so forth, because it makes one able to see them more clearly. There's a danger for anyone working like I do – that you become too obsessively involved with the picture to see it very clearly any longer. But I've never shown a picture thinking it's finished and then realised it wasn't.

And when things go wrong with a picture, you find that you can get it back?

That is perhaps the only part of my life as an artist about which I have total confidence. Most of my pictures have had nine, ten, twelve lives. But there's a marvellous sentimental remark in Muriel Spark's new book, where she says for an artist time can always be regained, wonders never cease. And of course it's true, because by an act of imagination you can always go back. Because when a picture of mine is going wrong it's when it's losing its meaning. But one can go back to the subject. That's the one thing I can do or the one thing I would claim I can do – I mean, even to the extent of going back to some love affair of long ago, or something like that. And, because for obvious reasons it was long ago and all gone, and so on, the picture might well then be almost completely dead and finished with. To turn it into a picture, one has to go back to the original feeling and then start making new bricks or rather new choices of bricks to build it up again. Somebody once said to me that I always claimed that my pictures were about feelings, whereas he thought they were always resolved in terms of the picture, in terms of pictorial language and in terms of the physical object. And he's quite right, because they are pictures and they have to be resolved in those terms. But the impetus for that resolution comes from the feeling, which is what they're about. And if I've succeeded, I've turned the original feeling, emotion, or whatever you like to call it, into an autonomous pictorial object, which I look at in exactly the same way you do. I once described finishing a painting to somebody as where – this is obviously talking of an ideal situation – the picture is somewhere hovering in mid-air between myself and the spectator so that it looks as strange or as interesting or whatever to me as it does to any other spectator.

II

Your subjects are very often social experiences, people sitting in their rooms talking, and so forth. Sometimes they have certain overtones of the comic or of the grotesque. But do you tend to paint subjects about people or situations where you're directly involved in a somewhat passionate way or rather situations in which you're fairly detached and something of an observer? Is there a tendency one way or the other?

Well, increasingly in recent years they are subjects in which I'm passionately and personally involved. I think my earlier pictures tended to be more voyeuristic than they've become. They're much more about myself now, or incidents which personally involved me, at least.

Do they tend to be more or less pleasurable experiences? Do they tend to be experiences which caused you anguish?

Well, both, really. There's a picture called *Reading the Letter*, which is in fact a picture about a very anguished and personally unpleasant experience – a letter written to someone else which, without being too specific about it, was very unpleasant for me to hear, and the picture is about the moment when it was being read aloud and I was in the room.

Do the subjects tend to be a single incident rather than something cumulative or composite?

When they're portraits of people they would be an accumulation of experiences of that person. But they're far more often particular moments of great pleasure or pain.

But just as often of pain as of pleasure?

No, less often pain, because those are not moments I particularly want to remember usually.

Except, of course, that there might be a motive to remember them in the possibility of catharsis through painting them.

Yes, there is that, and I think the picture I was talking about, *Reading the Letter*, probably was painted in part for that reason. There is another picture of that period that is totally voyeuristic and which is called *Tea*. And that was an extraordinary situation, because I went round to these friends to have tea and this person they hardly knew, who was a male prostitute, though they didn't seem to know that at the time, came round to see them, and we were making sort of ordinary fatuous social conversation and he said what do you do and I said I'm a painter, what do you do, and he said I'm a prostitute, and he seemed a very respectable and intelligent person and I said you must be joking, what do you mean you're a prostitute, and for the next six hours he described what his life as a prostitute was like. It was like something out of Mayhew's London. And nobody moved. I think that was the last voyeuristic painting I made.

What you've been saying about what has been happening in your painting is that it's become much more liberated, that you've been able to afford to put more of yourself into it.

That is quite true. I have been able to put more of myself into it.

And maybe that's why for me it's become increasingly moving.

And why there is more of it than there used to be.

Well, I expect it sounds patronising to talk like this, but I have to say that I've much admired your work since about 1960, but that in recent years it's made a great leap forward, as the Chinese say. And I think that you took off on that leap in 1975, especially in a painting called Grantchester Road.

I think that's true, and that it was when I was beginning to be able to join everything up together. Because my earlier pictures, I think, physically were very inorganic. It's not a word I like, but I can't think of another one. Like all artists who are alive now probably, I'm affected by assemblage and collage and the mixing of things, or rather the assembling of things, and the different elements in the language which I was talking about before didn't join. They remained too autonomous; I mean, their autonomy defeated to some extent the autonomy of the whole picture, or at least the physical identity of the whole picture. I saw last night a portrait of 1972 called *Interior 9AG*, which I hadn't seen for a very long time. I had terrible trouble with that picture and I resolved it eventually as a flat design, whereas now I would have used all kinds of illusionistic devices, which I do a little bit there, but in the end they're defeated by the pattern on the surface of the picture.

I don't say it was cause and effect and I don't know whether the chicken or the egg came first, but I think that at the time of that leap your key influence ceased to be Matisse and became early Vuillard, and I think that some of the marks and some of the variations and contrasts of marks that you're making now are like the kinds of marks – but blown up – that you get in Vuillard.

I've always been a fanatical admirer of Vuillard. As far as the influence of Matisse is concerned, I've always personally felt that his influence on me was not through his physical practice as an artist but his identity as artist, his moral identity as artist. His idea of how a twentieth-century artist lives and works influenced me far more than his actual practice as a painter. That doesn't mean that I don't deeply admire and enjoy his pictures, but I personally have never been able to see the physical influence of Matisse that everybody else seems to.

I don't see it in the work of recent years. I do very strongly see Vuillard of the Nineties. For example, there was a painting I was looking at in Zurich the other day of an interior with six figures, which seems terribly relevant to you. If one was doing a kind of placing of your work art-historically, I'd say that it's as if you'd taken these Vuillards and done two things to them: you've moved in, you've moved into close-up; and it's as if this flat, unbroken, unbreakable surface of a Vuillard had been deflowered.

I think that's exact (that's myself saying that as a spectator of what I've done). Funnily enough, just going back to dates and how my work has changed, after the second one-man show I ever had, which was in 1964, somebody wrote a piece about it where they described the pictures as a sort of brutalism of *intimisme*. So I think that it's a strain in my painting that has probably been there all along. But it's much more true now and it's become uppermost.

You talk about the use of illusionistic and space-making devices, and what I find remarkable about your work is that you do, as it were, penetrate, open, Vuillard's intact surface and create very mysterious and suggestive and cavernous spaces – possibly metaphors for orifices of the body, at times, especially in a painting called Day Dreams, *perhaps – and manage to do that without violating the flatness of the picture-plane.*

I take that as a great compliment and I think it's also extremely precise. But I only think so after the event, because one of the problems – as you've talked to so many artists, you must know all too well – one of the problems about talking about what one does is that one has to talk about it – at least I find that I have to talk about it – as a fellow spectator. I'm not just agreeing with you because I'm very pleased by what you say. I can also *see* it. But that's totally separate from what I'm thinking about when I'm working.

What are you thinking about when you're working?

I'm thinking about making illusionistic spaces.

But in making them, you don't lose the flatness of the picture-plane. I know that for me nothing in painting matters more than that an artist should be able to create an illusion of depth without disturbing the flatness of the picture surface, and that, if the sense of the surface is lost, looking at a picture makes me feel seasick. Dissolving the surface away is for me the sign of a bad artist – a bad artist even if in other ways he's as good as, say, Sargent. But I still don't understand intellectually why it matters so much.

Well, it's very simple, surely. It's a false position, it's a lie. I mean a picture, after all, is a flat thing, and all the mechanisms of *trompe l'oeil*, for example – this seems paradoxical at first but isn't really – depend on establishing the picture-plane. They don't work otherwise. Unless you first tell the spectator that he's looking at a flat thing, you can't otherwise make a hole in it. It's not for nothing that all those *trompe l'oeil* of dead game have wood-grain behind them – anything that will establish the surface. And I think that in Sargent's case it was almost a moral thing. He was an idle artist, and he didn't ever understand about the sort of simple rules of pictorial structure, and so the reason one feels seasick is because there's no ground. You aren't standing on anything solid.

Now, when you say that when you're painting you're thinking about how to make illusionistic spaces, is the preservation of the flatness of the surface instinctive or are you very consciously doing things to preserve it?

Invariably you have to, because, as I said earlier about all the mechanisms of *trompe l'oeil*, they won't work otherwise. You cannot produce a satisfactory illusion of depth without saying here is a flat surface, now we can open doors in it. And I disagree with the idea which is generally put forward that an obsession with the picture-plane is a twentieth-century thing.

It's absolute nonsense, when you think how obvious it is how Raphael or Titian worked to retain a sense of the surface.

It runs all through Old Master painting. You cannot have Baroque or Rococo constructions, which depend on illusion, without knowing absolutely where the picture-plane is and making quite certain that the spectator knows where it is too, which is the whole secret. We shouldn't need to be talking about this except that it's one of those extraordinary sorts of basic facts about making pictures which seem to get lost when not presented in ways that we're all familiar with.

III

When did you first go to India?

Well, I can't remember the date, but it must have been about sixteen years ago because I've been fourteen times. I like to go every year if I can.

Your interest in Indian art had developed before you went there?

Long before. I first became interested in Indian art as a child when I was about thirteen, and the first Indian paintings I saw astounded me because they depicted a whole world in a way which was completely convincing but totally separate from the tradition of Western art which I was used to. At least it seemed so at the time. I've realised long since that it wasn't nearly as separate as I first thought, but as it was a whole world in which everything was very precise and visible and yet somewhere else, I was very excited by this. And I think my main reason for going back to India is because it is somewhere else.

About the art, was it only paintings at first or was it textiles too?

No, it was just painting. I've become very interested in ornament of all sorts in the last few years, including Indian ornament, but not particularly. It's Indian painting that really continues to fascinate and obsess me.

It's an old truism that when you actually go to Umbria, for instance, you have the feeling that now you know what all those Umbrian paintings that you've seen are about. Have you been able to make that sort of connection in India?

Not at all, no. I once went on a very long and difficult journey to find a place where paintings in my collection were supposed to have been painted, and there was just a little village, and there was a landscape which seemed to have no connection at all with what appeared in the paintings. But it's the eclecticism of Indian painting which I think fascinated me right at the beginning. And I think that's because now, when the art that everybody practises is completely eclectic, to find such a totally and shamelessly eclectic art which was yet totally different – or so it seemed – from European painting was very exciting. And they seem to have an answer for everything. As a child I looked and I thought, how do you paint a tree? Well, they show you numerous ways of painting a tree, perhaps in the same picture.

Can you say what's taken you back to India again and again?

Because it was somewhere else. The friend I was travelling with in India this year, who himself goes often, was saying it's amazing how uncomfortable it is here, it's amazing how much one dislikes being here, so much is offensive and difficult for a Western person to contend with, why is it that we keep coming back? And it's a question I find almost impossible to answer. But it isn't just masochism, which one might think from that. It's just simply an atmosphere which is so totally different and yet is also so accessible, because people speak English and because their art, as I now have long since realised, uses so many of the conventions, but somehow the other way round or in some slightly distorted way, as well as sort of back to front. I mean they use all kinds of illusionistic devices that you find in Western art in a different way and somehow in a different sense, but they still use them. So you'll find continuous modelling, perspective, recession, changes of scale, changes of tone. And of course the picture-plane in Indian painting is inviolable, even in the worst pictures. They've never learnt how to break it.

Do you paint in India?

I did once. I once painted in India, and I produced this series of works on paper which I certainly would never be able to do again, under conditions of great hardship and a sort of Fascist situation. But they had to be done very, very quickly for technical reasons, extremely quickly, and so they're really a sort of distillation of years and years of going there, and they're very generalised in a way which I think does relate to certain kinds of rather low-grade Indian art.

How directly has the visual experience of India affected your painting?

I really don't know. I think that's easier for other people to see than for me to see. I think that looking at Indian paintings must have affected the language that I've used, but, looking at India itself, I wonder. The colours of the Indian landscape are rather like the colours of the landscape anywhere and people talk about the light in Greece or the light in Italy, or come to that, the light in upstate New York. I think that that's rather overrated. One can always find correspondences. I can walk out to the garden here on the night of a full moon and look at the dark sky and the dark trees and it might just as well be a garden in Delhi or Hyderabad or wherever. I think there is something, though, about those empty interiors on extremely hot afternoons and people lounging about on the vestigial furniture which probably has influenced me, but in a very tangential sort of way. It's more the moods, the way people live in India, that has probably influenced my painting very much . . . very much. It's the sort of nakedness of their usually very inhibited emotions. I mean, everything is very visible, somehow, there. Life isn't covered up with masses of objects, masses of possessions, so that the difference between being indoors or out of doors and all the sort of functions of life are much more visible, straightforward, than they are here.

There's a slowness of tempo in Indian life, an extreme slowness of tempo: there's also an extreme slowness of tempo in your painting.

That is true, and there's a sort of naked sensitivity about the people which probably affects me very much. But my life in India, you know, consists of living in hotels, seeing friends, suffering from dreadful smells and being most of the time curiously uncomfortable, and I don't think I can really explain what that does to my pictures. But earlier in this conversation you were talking about glimpses, and were starting to quote de Kooning. I don't know what you were going to say, but sometimes when I'm in India, unlike when I'm anywhere else, there are little glimpses when you see encounters between people – compared with the way we all behave, they behave with the utmost circumspection, and so forth. It has obviously influenced my painting a lot, come to think of it. Because there are glimpses of encounters and things that are like almost offstage, which suddenly impinge on you very clearly because of the general tempo of life there. There are sort of passionate moments. I don't mean mine, I've never had any passionate moments in India at all that I can recall; they've always been elsewhere. But you see them.

You started liking Indian painting at an early age. Did you become interested in collecting objects that you liked at an early age?

Oh, I've been a collector since I was about six.

Do you collect systematically within certain areas, or are you a magpie?

No, I'm not at all a magpie, quite the opposite. And I've always thought that if I got something very good, if I had anything like it that was less good, it should leave at once.

And what are the areas in which you've collected over the years?

Really, mainly Indian paintings. I always wanted to have a great piece of European sculpture and I made many unsuccessful attempts. I did finally buy a piece, but I never had enough money to buy things that I wanted, and still probably the best Indian painting I have, I had to sell my entire collection to buy. And so my collection has remained very small, but it has got better and better as time's gone on. And I now also collect Indian drawings, which are a great passion of mine.

And textiles?

I have a collection of Mughal carpet fragments and I've got one whole carpet, but that's because I've become interested in ornament.

So all your collecting has been Indian, from the very start?

I've never tried to collect anything else with any sort of passion. The first Indian paintings I bought were when I was thirteen. I bought two Indian miniatures, which I couldn't afford, and I borrowed some money to bet on a horse race to pay for them and of course lost it all. I managed in the end by selling one of the pictures to pay for them both. And since then I've bought really seriously only Indian paintings. But I've decided to stop. Next year I'll be fifty, and I think I can probably buy the two pictures which will complete my collection, and then I shall just stop, because I think it's something I can't continue dealing with. It's an emotional strain. It's another emotional strain I think I'm too old to contend with.

Do you keep the things out where you can see them or do you keep them put away so that you take them out to look at them?

Nearly all my collection is on loan at the V&A. I think that's the first step in stopping collecting. I lent them to them three years ago, and a great friend of mine said: as soon as you empty your shelves you'll fill them again. And it's quite true. I've made another collection since I lent those.

Also Indian?

Mostly of Indian drawings, yes, but I don't look at them very often. I hang them on the wall, but I find after a bit I don't look at them. So what I like to do from time to time is hang the lot of them up and look at them and spend a lot of time looking at them and then take them down again.

Are you obsessive about the way you hang your collection?

Absolutely. That's why I got rid of it. I found that I was getting too worried about it. Until about three weeks ago my bedroom in this house had Indian pictures hanging all around it and the relief now at waking up in the morning and just looking out of the window when the walls are bare is tremendous. So I think that's another step.

Does your interest in displaying things extend to hanging your own exhibitions when you can?

I care desperately about that. One of the reasons why I have no London gallery at the moment is because I got so concerned about the space in which I was going to show my pictures. And I changed galleries in New York because I wanted to go to a room which I thought was the right one.

IV

I think for obvious reasons I will never succeed, but I would like to be a classical painter, or classical artist I would rather say, where all emotion, all feeling, turns into a beautifully articulated anonymous architectural memorial at the other end. I think that that's what my pictures are attempting to do, and that's why I want the language to be as impersonal as possible. So I'm trying to make a harmonious impersonal structure, but unfortunately I'm beginning dimly to realise that the marks I make are not as impersonal or autonomous as I'd really like them to be. It's a major concern of mine that every mark that I put down should not be a piece of personal autograph but just a mark, which then can be used with any other to contain something. I want to make marks that are anonymous as well as autonomous. They can't be one without the other, it seems to me; otherwise, they would remind you of somebody's handling.

Tell me of an artist who particularly attracts you for making marks that are not autograph.

Jacques-Louis David, who, in some of his female portraits, very deliberately left them loose in a way which prefigures the painting by Degas we've been talking about and who, particularly when he was painting the backgrounds, used a totally mechanical circular motion of the brush, which makes a network, which makes a surface. It established a plane: then he would smudge little bits over. That seems to me a perfectly good example of non-autograph.

1982

And marks that are autograph and that you rather wish were not?

Manet is the obvious example, and of course he used them in such a sort of magic manner. When it works it's fine, but there are times when his pictures are not at their greatest, when I find that the autograph marks are made to stand in for something that could perhaps have a little more meaning. Because the trouble with autograph marks is that they look as if they mean something. They're like scribbled signatures where actually they're not real. This sounds very moralistic, but the trouble with autograph marks in the end is that they physically or pictorially seem to work but they don't really mean anything. I don't think in the end there's much difference between them, because the non-autograph mark has to be given meaning just like an autograph one has to, but I think it's a more straightforward operation if the mark is as simple and direct as possible.

What do you think of Jasper Johns's marks?

Well, I think that Jasper makes a lot of different kinds of marks. He does make autonomous and impersonal marks, I think, with tremendous success. Where they fail to be that is where he wants – which is, I think, one of the most difficult things to do, but which I also try to do – to make, as it were, emotive-type marks but in quotation marks, so that they're not in fact emotive, they're just that kind of mark. If he does that in his drawings sometimes, I think, very unsuccessfully, it's because it's very difficult to build in quotation marks, it's very difficult to build in our ironical bit, in terms of actual handling, and he does try and do that. I think in his paintings and in his best prints he certainly succeeds in making marks which are emotive and cold all at once. Lucky man. We've all long been taught to believe that certain kinds of physical marks have one meaning and others have another, so that, to put it at its most simplistic, a loose mark is romantic and imprecise and a hard mark or a sharp one is classical and architectural. It's not actually true, but it's a tremendous barrier one has to jump over. Don't you think Jasper's trying very hard to do that? And I'm also trying.

I think in any case that you're one of the painters whose marks are really peculiar to themselves. I think they have a very haunting sense of mystery and a kind of slightly disarrayed luxury.

113

I restrict myself deliberately to very few kinds of marks. Astonishingly few, really. Hardly any modelling, as you've probably noticed, except, as it were, in inverted commas. Phoney *trompe l'oeil* modelling; spots, stripes, but not lines. Trying to avoid, as far as possible, any overtly linear marks, so that each mark itself can be autonomous, because, as soon as you draw a line round something, already the line itself is not autonomous: it's enclosing a shape and it's got an inside and an outside. At one time I thought I'd become a completely Pointillist painter: a dot or a stripe is something over which one has infinitely more control than something which depends on the movement of the arm, which takes you back into autograph. To be an artist now, you have to make your own language, and for me that has taken a very long time. Gradually, as you make your own language, the more you learn to do, the more you can do, and the more you include.

I think you now include a much greater richness of metaphor and that this has come about through the risks you've been taking by opening up space. What I'd like you to tell me is how conscious you are, or think you are, of making metaphors. I mean, I'm never sure how much painters push metaphor in their work. I don't think it's necessarily a bad thing to do so. It's obvious that Picasso is an artist very consciously involved in making metaphors, though he also obviously made them unconsciously. But I think that some artists can create rich metaphors without thinking about it at all. I imagine that an artist like Bonnard, whose work is rich in metaphor, would be trying to deal with particular experiences quite specifically, letting the metaphors come of their own accord.

I think I would be somewhere between those two extremes, because I think that Bonnard is, in the terms that you have just been describing, which I think are exact, the opposite to Picasso.

I think that Braque in the Ateliers *is using metaphors in a very conscious way. I don't mean a disastrously conscious way.*

No, but in a totally conscious way. But I would have said that in my own case, it's a position I am forced into by the nature of the subject-matter, rather than its being a conscious decision. There are many aspects of the subjects which I paint pictures about that would lose their meaning if they were too specifically presented, and that's why I am forced into metaphor. That's one reason, but others are the nature of my language and the nature of the pictorial object I end up with. I'm forced into the use of metaphors, because, if you particularise too much, especially about private emotions, they would remain in the painting. In fact, the more I think about this, my pictures are totally metaphorical, but in a way that is of necessity rather than by design. The total difference between the metaphor in my work and, say, Braque's, which you mentioned, is that his, I think, is ultimately in terms of architecture, it's about pictorial problems to start with, whereas I begin with an emotional situation which I've got to make physical in terms of the pictorial, in terms of the picture, and I've got to turn into pictorial architecture in some way. Whereas I think that in Braque's *Ateliers*, which I think are great works and infinitely his greatest pictures, the original impetus probably, and this is only making a very loose description, is pictorial and has to do with pictorial architecture. But the pictorial architecture in my pictures comes from a metaphor for emotion.

HARRISON BIRTWISTLE 2001

Recorded in June 2001, just a few days before David Sylvester died, in his house in London. Edited in collaboration with Harrison Birtwistle, who writes, 'David came back into my life after a long time, and for the last ten years we had what I felt was a sort of intellectual love affair – his death has made a great hole in my life, and in everybody's, even though they did not know him, and may not realise this.'

DAVID SYLVESTER *Are you busy writing a new piece?*

HARRISON BIRTWISTLE Well, it's a nocturne, and it's sort of an attempt at the ultimate nocturne.

What size of orchestra – big?

Big orchestra, yes, and the nice thing about writing slow music is that it doesn't require so many notes, you know, and I'm having to be brave at not being intimidated or seduced into making it faster, keeping my cool, as it were, for a piece that's slow from beginning to end. You know, the contrast is of a different order, isn't it, when it's all slow. I mean, tempo can't really come into it.

Yes. What will be your ideal so far of the nocturne in the sense of persistent slowness? Something by Morton Feldman?

Well, that's the first thing that comes to mind, but that is too obvious because the whole question of contrast in that sense wasn't an issue with him. I'm not quite the same. So this is really an attempt to write a piece which is in a terminal state of beginning, if that makes any sense.

Is there anything similar in earlier music?

Well, in a way, everything in earlier music is like that. It's to do with the whole question of decisions, in that if you listen to a piece of Beethoven, you can, in a sense, understand the moves, even if they are brilliantly calculated. But in a lot of earlier music, say pre-Renaissance/Renaissance music, which I am particularly interested in, you can't really understand what the journey was, what the decisions were.

I've been fascinated by this piece of Machaut all my life and it's a piece, it's a hocket – that means a 'hiccup', the passing over of voices to different instruments, so that it becomes fractured – it's a medieval technique. It's in three parts and for me it speaks like no other music because in one sense there is a very structured game going on . . . you know, it's a bit like someone watching cricket, who doesn't know at all that there is something with a lot of rules which are sort of incomprehensible but nevertheless structured. Does that make sense?

Yes.

So the whole question of continuity is of a different order. You see with tonality, you know there is this sort of inner logic. You know you go through a procedure and you actually know when you come to the end. That's why a lot of late nineteenth-century music, Brückner, Mahler – in this overtly tonal music, particularly in Brückner, the piece ends a long time before it finishes. I mean, I listened to a Brückner symphony recently in the Festival Hall, and the piece ended and I looked at my watch and logically to my ears it had finished, it was twenty past, I remember – I don't know what hour, but it was twenty past, and it was still finishing at twenty to.

(Laughs) Because it was still . . .

Because it had come to its logical end . . . and it was simply being spun out, to my ears. That sort of thing works very well in the opposite direction. You take the beginning of *Rheingold* – Wagner understood that, but it's at the coda where there is a problem, because I suppose in the enunciation there is always the expectancy of something to happen.

This is about continuity and non-continuity and – if you don't have tonality – whether there is a different sort of continuity, and where the continuity comes from. You know, I very often hear music written this century which is not in a key that aids tonality – it goes through the motions of tonality. That to me is a fake, it's a sort of fake continuity, it's remembered continuity. But music is something we're sort of conditioned to, in the way that it speaks, and that is why in modern music there are terrible problems, for the audience, about comprehensibility.

Well, yes, understanding the logic of why one thing follows another.

Whereas with tonal music, the logic is very, very clear.

Well, there's an inner logic, there's a sub-structure of tonality really, where that carries you forward. Now in the case of Beethoven, to my ears, there are many surprises, many things are set up and he never ever quite does what you think he's going to do and the funny thing about it is, to me they're always surprises even if I know they're coming. It's to do with repetition, it's to do with the thing of what you set up and then don't fulfil.

Tonality was the great armature of music, but then we became free from it. That has been what I've tried to articulate, I've tried to make another sort of continuity and work out how things can properly speak in another way, because we're free from this thing. So in one way tonality serves the continuity, but in another way it chains it; it's the thing that held it together, and that's why it all broke down.

And when did it break down?

Oh, it broke down before Schoenberg.

Precisely where, in Wagner?

In moments of Wagner and moments of Strauss. And at the beginning of, for instance, the opening of the last movement to Mahler's First Symphony. To me this is a remarkably radical piece. I think for its time it was completely extraordinary, but time is the great leveller, isn't it, and we became familiar with these things. Also, if you think of the extraordinary thing of what Wagner did with *The Ring*, when you think of what happened before, there is nothing quite like it. I mean, it's an enormous idea, all based on a single idea as well, which is delightful too.

We know all the tunes, you know – that is the structure of the theme.

Entirely composed of leitmotifs?

Yes.

And that had never been done before.

Well, not that I know of. Certainly not in the same way. So the inner logic of the tunes is being structured by the dramatic thrust.

When you say the dramatic structure, does that mean that it's something that could only happen in opera, or could it happen in symphonic music . . .?

Oh yes, it can, of course it can . . . But the thing about tonality is that it was something that was taken for granted and you didn't have to think about it. The harmonic, the fundamental harmonic cycle, is the same in Beethoven as it is in inferior music, the cycle of fifths and the genius of Beethoven is how he transcended that.

Before the introduction of the leitmotif, what is the previous comparably radical transformation of the language?

All the things, I suppose, that came out of dance forms. Do you mean of that period, or do you mean before Beethoven?

Before Wagner; what before Wagner is the last equally huge or comparably huge transformation?

Oh, the life of Beethoven. I mean, he started with something which he was born with – Mozart, roughly speaking – and made something completely radical within the framework of tonality. The radical quality was harmony more than anything, the way that he moved into the scheme . . . You know this is not really my subject in the sense, you know, that you might ask a musicologist. I've been a sort of observer of it. I'm something of a magpie.

Are you?

Yes, in my understanding of it. I find that when I was a performer – I was a clarinettist – I played a huge amount of music which just, as it were, you would hear from a very different perspective in the orchestra and from your particular part, your relationship with it, and you are isolated in the piece. It's a very strange thing. So I am very familiar, incredibly familiar is the word, with a lot of classical music and I'm always surprised when I haven't really heard something for a long time at just how well I know it.

In Vienna last year I went to a performance of Beethoven's Fourth Symphony with Claudio Abbado and the Vienna Phil and I hadn't heard it for years, but in the light of the music that I've written over the last thirteen years, I was listening to it from a very different point of view. I knew it well, but my priorities at what I was isolating and what I was impressed by were completely different. I was very taken, for instance, by the use of the bassoon, which had never occurred to me before. The use of the bassoon in the Fourth Symphony is extraordinary because I think Beethoven identified something in the instrumental voice of the bassoon that had never been identified before. He understood the lyric quality of the instrument. I don't know whether there is anything in the history of music where the bassoon has lyrical quality or is used in that way. I don't know whether there is a precedent for that, for it to be used as a melodic instrument. It's allotted very important material and I find that absolutely extraordinary to write this incredible piece, to start writing one of the great pieces – and to allot some of this wonderful music to this instrument – to actually identify its melodic quality.

Does that happen in painting with colour?

What, that you're identifying colour? Well, this is your territory. You see, I suppose that colours are changeable. I mean, if you go to Windsor & Newton and you don't mix something, if one painter just puts a colour on the canvas from the same tube as another one, very often, very quickly it doesn't become the same picture, it changes. But the other thing in the programme which struck me too is that this is about instrumental role-play, you know, allotting material to the voice of an instrument irrespective of the material it's playing, so that it's like a character in a play . . . it's a voice. The context can change, but the voice is the same.

But also in the programme was the Beethoven fiddle concerto. I'm telling you this because it was the first real concert of classical music that I went to which moved me a great deal for these reasons: I was listening to it as a composer who has been writing music for thirty years or thereabouts, maybe longer, a long time. But have you ever weighed up how the material is allotted to the solo violin in the Beethoven fiddle concerto? I mean, to begin with it doesn't play and then it plays an accompaniment and it's a long, long way into the piece if you listen to it in this way, before it actually plays melodic material.

How do you relate these discoveries to your famous remark that it would be desirable to have a moratorium on everything from Haydn to Brahms for a certain number of years in order to refresh people's musical consciousness? But I suppose you perhaps in a sense had your own inner moratorium, in that you have taught much more and listened much more to earlier and later music. And you yourself have now come back fresh to the great classics.

Yes, I have. It's as if I've been saving them up and I've learnt something, because I can actually hear them in a different way. I think there are priorities of listening. I mean, that's what Sheila always said about my music, that when she hears it for the second time it's never the same piece. She said, you know, 'Is that the piece I heard before?' and then the third time she said, 'You know, that sounds completely different again.' I think that's because the priorities by which you listen, the ways you listen to music, change. Consequently if you're writing complex textures, as I do, I think that probably does come into it.

Also the concentration thing. The whole question of music is to do with memory, you know, because that's the way we carry information forward; we need something by which we have to remember things and, in the end, it is repetition. There are certain things which are taken on and which sort of seem to be there or have been developed for various reasons. It's a very self-conscious thing that I've done, it's to do with repetition, because repetition is concerned really with time.

And how do you as a composer feel about your audience? Is your audience helping you, hindering you, or is it neutral? Are you aware of how your music is heard? How it is listened to? And does it matter to you?

What I would like my audience to get from it is what I get from it. What I put into it is what I want to be heard. But the problem with music relates back to repetition, in a different sense – I mean, you can become familiar with anything by repetition, just any sound or noise, whatever. So it really comes back to this tonality question: even if you heard a Beethoven symphony that you never heard before, there would be certain things that you would be familiar with. You know, there is something, a structure underneath by which you would understand. It would speak to you. And to come back to him again, his genius is how he changed these things, within this pattern that we are familiar with or accustomed to, and understand to be 'true to life' – how he transcended it.

You talked before about comprehensibility. I'm going to say something which may be very foolish. With classical music, part of the emotional satisfaction that I get from the music is that I understand what is happening and the very act of understanding moves me. With certain modern music – for example, your own – I don't understand what is happening and one of the things which moves me is the fact that I don't *understand. It's the mystery of it. I mean, emotionally it produces strong gut reactions and I suspect that these are enhanced by my lack of understanding of what's going on. Is that nonsense?*

No, it's not nonsense. But this question of expectancy and using it as a means of setting certain things up, I think this is the crux. This is the thing in Beethoven – you see we're using him, as a metaphor, because he's the best one at it again, or as an emblem, I should say.

He never quite does what you think he's going to do, and he's always in the light of this tonal journey. He always shows you the byways and builds expectancy as if saying, 'Well, you know there is this thing' – because we know there are certain core progressions – but he sets it up and it is never quite what you expect. I saw *Fidelio* the other day, an extraordinary piece, it's like nothing else in its relationship with text and the secondary material. There's no tunes in it, that's the other thing. It's full of wonderful melodic invention, but there's nothing like the overture.

You're saying that in Fidelio *the opera, there's nothing quite like the tunes in the overture?*

Yes, that's right.

Ah-ha. Well, who are the tune-rich composers? Is Tchaikovsky rich in tune?

Probably. Well, it's a nineteenth-century invention, isn't it?

'When I am laid in earth', *isn't that? No, that's not a tune.*

Well, it's melodic. I mean it's exquisite melody.

Did Cole Porter write great tunes?

Yes.

Did the Beatles write great tunes?

One or two, one or two. Schubert does write tunes. And great melodies. But I think they sort of get in the way of developmental thought, symphonic thought.

Do you think, going back to my proposition that one can be moved by music through feeling that one understands it, or through feeling one doesn't understand it, do you think that is valid or not?

My problem is, in the way you're thinking, that I don't have any problem with music. I don't have it, I don't. You know, one of the most difficult pieces is that cavatina string quartet of Beethoven's. And that has no theme at all, at all, just melody, and that is a good example of a problem piece and, to me, I think I find it quite straightforward in a way. I mean, I think it's absolutely magical and mysterious and of an order of invention that doesn't exist anywhere else. It's a unique piece. I think that he probably wrote more unique pieces than anyone.

Yes. Undoubtedly. Do you feel that he knew how he was doing? . . . I mean, I have a feeling, for example, that painters often don't know what they're doing; that, for example, the so-called development of Analytical Cubism to

Synthetic Cubism . . . I do think that Picasso and Braque didn't know what they were doing.

But I think there is a difference, because the thing about Cubism is that more has been written about Cubism than anything else because it's analytical, because you can analyse it. But if you put yourself in front of a painting and imagine you are the person who is doing it, I think you would feel they knew *what* they were doing, but I don't think they knew *why* they were doing it. I think they knew what they were doing.

I say all the time that I've no idea what I'm doing, you know, because it's all about a sort of personal coherence. It's about the way that one thing develops out of another, how you can simply stop something, and push something up against it that is not related. Very often I worry a great deal in that one thing is just as good as another. It seems to me, at the time that I'm doing it, that any goddamn thing will do. And, whenever I have a solution to anything, it seems that I always want to walk away from it, and then I don't know if I've forgotten the solution. I don't know why. I can only believe in something in the way that I . . . I can only believe in the idea, if it's a spontaneous thing. And if I leave an idea as it were, pin it on the board, whatever – if only you could do that with music – and then come back to it, I can never take it off the board and just do it. I have to re-create that moment where it seems like a sort of answer. It's logical for that moment and can only be for that moment. So maybe, you know, one throws away good ideas in the dustbin full of great ideas.

MICHAEL BREARLEY 2001

Recorded in David Sylvester's London house on 21 April 2001, six weeks before his death, this interview is a typically passionate and energetic affirmation of his enjoyment of life, art and cricket. It has been edited by Michael Brearley and is published here for the first time.

DAVID SYLVESTER *This interview is meant to focus on a topic – the differences and likenesses between the aesthetics of sports and the aesthetics of arts. You're peculiarly qualified to talk about these, first because you've been a professional sportsman and a successful captain of your country, second that you're a professional psychoanalyst, and third that you spend a great deal of your time as a consumer of the arts, all of them.*

As a point of departure, the other day I heard a phrase used by a television announcer giving notice of various sports programmes. Out of the blue he said, 'Timing, that's what sport is about – timing.' This made me ask myself whether this remark was a truism?

MICHAEL BREARLEY Timing. If you play a sport, if you play a stroke as a batsman or bowl a ball as a bowler, timing is of the essence. There is an exquisite feeling attached to timing a ball perfectly, which is one of the deep reasons for playing sport. It is the moment when you get something exactly right. But it isn't only a matter of timing; there's also placing. Full satisfaction in a stroke or delivery happens when timing and placing are both just right. Another element is repeatability. It is all very nice to time a shot right, but it's even nicer to feel one is doing it reliably, as well. I remember playing a shot off [Gary] Sobers when the ball went like a rocket to the cover boundary, timing and placing both perfect, but actually I knew it was a fluke. I let my hands go in the direction of the ball, with minimal footwork, and just happened to hit it sweetly past the fielder so that it bounced back off the wooden fence. The pleasure would have been greater had there been more control, more sense that I might do it again when an opportunity arose.

You're talking about timing and placing. You're talking about the aesthetic satisfaction which the poet gets, I take it, from finding exactly the right word for that rhyme, the word that you need for that line at that moment. You get the feeling that it's the only possible word. My question here is: to what extent is that experience echoed in the spectator? How does the spectator's pleasure in seeing it relate to the performer's pleasure in doing it? And does the painter, when he does it with a stroke of the brush, get that same satisfaction?

Well, you'd have to tell me the answer to that last question. But I imagine he does. I imagine there must be something similar when, after a struggle, one finds the right thing. But as to your other question, yes, certainly in sport, the spectator picks up that satisfaction. There are two essential points of view in the aesthetics of sport, which you've raised at once: that of the performer and that of the spectator. I think the latter engages with, identifies with, and dis-identifies with the agent in the sport in a way parallel to what happens when we look at a picture. In a certain way, the viewer is freer than the player because of the distance and detachment, which enables him to have a full range of thoughts and imaginings, whereas the player is pressed in upon by the exigencies of the next ball or flow of the game. Indeed, one mistake a batsman makes is to be carried away by his own excellent form. In your own writing on art you take advantage of this freedom and space to identify and then dis-identify from the painter's activity. You allow yourself to imagine what he might have been up to. You also come back to the particular viewpoint of the watcher. A similar experience is available to the attentive spectator of sport.

Certainly watching sport gives people an experience of utter absorption in an event. I saw a picture in a Sunday newspaper recently. A footballer had just headed the ball, which was on its way into the goal. The football was in the foreground, but not in close focus. What was in focus was a section of the crowd. I was impressed by the intent expressions on every face. Not one, of perhaps a hundred people, was looking elsewhere. Each face expressed pure concentration; there was no smiling, no yawning, no boredom, no distraction, no anger. Simply absorption in this dramatic moment. This comes close to what one sometimes experiences as a viewer of a work of art or drama on the stage. These football spectators may identify with the scorer; or with the defender who has failed to reach the ball in time. But they also occupy a more neutral position. Incidentally, such a shifting of viewpoints is not unlike what I do in my work as a psychoanalyst. In that role I am constantly drawn by the patient to see things from his point of view. And this is essential . . . But I also need to dis-identify from this, and identify with others in the story that the patient is telling. I must also inhabit my own point of view, as his interlocutor.

In art criticism there's room for an imaginative consideration of how the model is being used in the making of a painting, how the painter treats her visually. This opens up reflection on how she or he might feel in relation to such a mode of looking. (A crucial part of work with patients in psychoanalysis is how the patient feels looked at.) The critic/viewer enlarges his take on the picture by standing imaginatively in the shoes of painter, painted and spectator.

When a goal is scored, there is a mixture of placing and timing. As the spectator, there's no doubt that one's own reactions and the reactions of the scorer and of other players are almost identical. It's that mixture of placing and timing that causes the goalkeeper to miss the ball. He dives a millisecond too early or a millisecond too late. It can be either – we see penalties scored when the goalkeeper dives too early, and the guy shooting the goal puts the ball where he had just been. It's a mixture of timing and placing. In a painting, we get this tremendous satisfaction that a mark is in exactly that place and no other. Now, the first thing you did when I talked about timing was to bring in placing. My question is: can we talk about timing as distinct from placing? Are we not talking about placing/timing rather as if we were talking about space/time? Are spacing and timing not the same?

Well, no, they're not. There is a space difference between playing a perfectly timed cover drive straight to a fielder; and next ball I play exactly the same shot, but three yards to his right. The latter gives me more satisfaction, but the timing might be identical.

Ah, and this is the key question. Is the timing the same? Isn't that placing completely tied up with the timing? Is the shot in fact perfectly well-timed if it goes straight to the fielder? Does the batsman feel the same satisfaction in his muscles when that happens?

I think he does. But he's disappointed as well.

He's disappointed, but is the feeling, the physical feeling, the same?

I think I have two answers here. One is yes, it often is. I play the shot, feel the pleasure, look up and am delighted or frustrated as the case may be. The other is when I have the picture of the field-setting properly in mind, and subliminally adjust my shot just right, so it bisects the fielders. Then the full aesthetic pleasure, in muscles and mind, is as you suggest. But the other situation is common enough. In golf each action is simply you and the ball [**DS**: *Yes*] and the hole. You play a shot and you hit it dead right. You get that feeling through your hands of perfect timing, you look up and you think: O God, it's too high, or too far, it was the wrong club, it's in the bunker. You don't lose the feeling because the outcome is not the desired one. Perhaps there's a difference between the ordinary player and the top pro, though I'm not sure.

Well, this is crucial because, when I made the analogy with the brush mark that's in the right place, if it's not in the right place, then what the hell is the timing?

The funny thing about a painting is that although you can see it from different angles and from different distances, once finished, it exists in a timeless way. It might deteriorate, and so on, but it's there, that's it. From the point of view of the end product, does it matter how it was constructed? Or is this an ignorant remark?

Think again, because this is the crux.

Well, the point I'm trying to make is that with a painting the thing you've got exists in space, but doesn't change through time. A piece of music obviously changes over time. A cricket stroke exists in time and place. You could take a photograph or film of a batsman without including the fielder; he's playing a perfectly correct stroke. And you could be sure of that, and agreeably pleased by that, without having to know whether the ball goes past the fielder or straight to him. In sport, as in drama, you'd have to see it in time.

In drama?

Yes.

The exact moment of Oedipus' realisation of what has happened, the timing of that moment, is what is crucial. It is the timing of that moment of discovery.

Yes. But in the staging of it, you'd have to think of where to put the characters on the stage. In your memory of seeing the play you'd see it in space as in time. You would remember how the stage was, you'd have the whole geography of it in mind. So I don't know, I think there might be a difference between the space/time framework of sport and drama, and the time framework of music, and the space framework of art. But I don't know how to take that further at the moment.

Well, there is a point here which may be relevant. Of course, in music, a good example of timing is rubato. Whether the player gets the rubato right or wrong decides whether it comes out sounding poignant or sentimental – that's timing. And it's absolutely crucial to the writing and to the performance, or to the combination of the two. But what I wanted to ask you – and this may be where sport and art are profoundly different – is: are art and sport profoundly different in that in sport there is a result, in a work of art there is no result? In sport there is a difference between the shot that produces four runs, and the one that produces none because cover point stops it. The result counts.

Yes, I agree, that is a difference. And this may be partly why sportsmen characteristically underplay the aesthetic. They talk in terms of cost-effectiveness. They sneer at pretty play. Now of course one would sneer at pretty art as well, one might do that.

Yes, exactly, exactly.

But the sportsman would ask: 'How many runs could you get for that shot?' I learnt a lesson many years ago, when I played a pretty late cut against an off-spinner. The ball turned, kept low and hit my off-stump. M. J. K. Smith, the England captain at that time, asked me, tactfully,

'How many runs would you have got if you'd played that shot exactly right?' I said, 'One', and he said, 'So was it worth it?' You see what I mean? If the stroke would have been worth four if I'd played it properly, it just might have been worth the risk. But despite what I said before, aesthetics enters into this value-for-money business.

Go on.

If a batsman shovels a ball through mid-wicket in an ungainly way, with a lot of bottom hand, and manages to time it and place it right and the ball goes for four, this doesn't give us (or the batsman) the same satisfaction as seeing Viv Richards, say, stroking the same ball through the same space, imperiously, with a sense of inevitability. And the reason for this satisfaction is partly that it is beautifully done, but also that it's more reliable. As a spectator or player you say to yourself, 'Ah, that man can play the shot at will.' I've known bowlers who dreaded bowling against Viv. But with the first man, the shoveller, you might as a bowler think, 'I'll try that again, a bit slower, and he might well miss it.' Cost-effectiveness is related to classical form or correctness of form. We can see intuitively that with a straight bat you're more likely to make contact with the ball than if you play across the line, or with a crooked bat.

I think I'm making a rather complicated point. First there is this element of outcome that enters into how we enjoy and appreciate sport, which is lacking in a work of art. Nevertheless – second point – our pleasure in that outcome is partly aesthetically based. Classic form develops for the purpose of reliable effectiveness. There is a third point, which I touched on before, and that is that when a batsman has the whole field-placing in his mind, and is able to put the ball exactly where he wants to, this gives pleasure to him and to the spectator.

Beautiful. But if so, what is the art equivalent of cost-effectiveness?

I've tried to think about that and I don't know that there is one. There must be limitations in any medium. There must be difficulties in expressing what one wants to in that medium. Is part of what we appreciate in art to do with making the best of a bad job? Making something that should work against you work for you?

I'm not forgetting this point about cost-effectiveness, but maybe we can get at it in this way. The other day I was watching a Sri Lankan batsman playing some good spin bowling and playing it with beautiful correctness. I was responding to the sheer correctness of his straight bat. Was that pleasure an academic intellectual recognition, or was it an aesthetic response to the correctness?

Yes, O Socrates!

Both.

I think so.

It's not something that you would only recognise if you'd been coached as a schoolboy and learnt how you're supposed to play?

No, but you'd have to know the game. Just as you have to know something about painting to appreciate a work. You can't just listen to Bartók or Beethoven, or look at Pollock, say, and understand it without knowing something. Similarly with a game. Knowing something about cricket might not be coached, it might be learnt just from watching or playing in the streets.

It might be learnt from watching?

Yes, it might.

But then it would feed back to effectiveness?

It would. The two are indissolubly linked. There would be many other factors besides correctness in our appreciation. I too saw some of the recent Sri Lanka–England series on television, and I loved watching England's Graham Thorpe bat. He played many classical shots, both defensive and attacking. But what he also was able to do was take a calculated chance, as a deliberate ploy. When Muralitharan, the great Sri Lankan spin bowler, bowled vastly turning leg-breaks to him as a left-hander, Thorpe would occasionally plant his front foot down the pitch, and smite the ball over mid-wicket against the spin. He would play these unorthodox strokes for a specific purpose, as part of a strategy. He did it to persuade bowler and captain to take away a close catcher, and put him on the mid-wicket boundary. If you saw this shot out of context, you'd say it was a cow-shot, too risky. You'd hope the youngsters weren't watching. But in fact it was an exceptionally good piece of batting. The result was that Thorpe would be free to work ones and twos by pushing the ball with minimal risk into the big open spaces on the leg side. I thought he outwitted the opposition captain by this willingness to take a risk. These were big shots, on which a lot depended. That is an important part of batting skill.

But in painting and music too, one of our great excitements lies in our response to risk.

I agree.

If the composer or painter can bring it off, risk makes it all more exciting. Risk in art and risk in sport are very close.

Yes, I agree. And in both activities there is the need to balance out risk and safety.

You know that a painter could have chosen an easier solution to resolve a compositional problem, but if he chooses the easier one, there won't be the same frisson.

Yes. You know, there's another interplay, closely related but different, which these examples remind me of, and that's the one between spontaneity and planning. I'm reminded of the remark attributed to the old Nottinghamshire cricketer, George Gunn, that 'Most batsmen pay too much attention to the bowling. They don't go with the tide.' If you're batting at your best, there is a constant oscillation between absorption and relaxation, of freedom and at the same time prudence, care, planning. Thorpe's risk was based on a definite decision; he set himself to do just that when the ball was in the right spot, he'd worked out that the risk was worth the gamble. But at other times he would just do something without conscious planning or thinking. Even in the state I've described, he was on the go, on the look-out for a chance to do something different. Even in this mind-set there's this combination of conscious and unconscious. Donald Tovey, the music historian and critic, made the same point when he said that if you asked the centipede to concentrate on each of its legs, and move each one intentionally, it would immediately fall into the ditch. But at the same time, there will have been hours of focused attention on each finger's movements for a violinist, say. I imagine there is an analogy to having a game plan for an innings, or in having a strategy in the field, to art.

Of course. But the question is, do we actually get an aesthetic excitement as spectators from responding to that planning?

I think the answer is, potentially yes. It's part of what the discerning spectator finds enjoyable. You can observe a batsman building an innings, going through the immense struggle of the early stages, let's say. You can see him gradually opening up, having phases in his innings, and you can get satisfaction in that.

Such as you get from seeing a Henry Moore, or from reading a Henry James?

Yes, the intelligence behind writing, behind the work . . .

And the aesthetic satisfaction you get from the intelligence behind the writing.

Yes, exactly. One gets a sense of the person going about his work, doing his job. You describe this in some of your work. You imaginatively evoke how a painter has produced this thing that you have in front of you, what sort of processes may have gone on, and sometimes you confirm this by conversation with him. This leads into the range of human qualities one can perceive in someone's performance. Courage is an obvious example. In sport it's very obvious.

Of course, you can see this in the way a group of actors works together as a team, it's like a team in sport. And you watch the interplay of those actors.

That's right. And you get a sense of the director too, sometimes.

And a sense of the director. Absolutely.

I don't know how much that team effort applies in art, where the work is usually done by someone on his own.

It's something you get more of a sense of in collaborative art. Yes. We've been talking away about timing, ostensibly. What do we really mean when we say that the timing was perfect? Are we to apply it to making love? There are changes of rhythm when you're making love, which happen through the spontaneous interaction of two people, which give them both greater satisfaction. And there's a sense of the two together working towards an end. Is timing in love-making closely analogous – I think it is – to timing in the arts and sports?

It's an interesting analogy. You bring in one of the most intimate two-person activities in life. A baby at the breast is another one.

Yes.

But the timing that we think of in sport is often both momentary and done by a single person in response to a challenge from an opponent. There's also the timing of a whole innings, or in the lengthening of stride in the last lap of a race, when a runner beautifully surges past his rivals with something to spare. But as I say, these are individual activities. It's not quite two people together. In a football team, players collaborate, and incisive and intricate passing movements call for perfect timing between players. I suppose one might try to include partnerships between batsmen and bowlers, but that's stretching it a bit. I'm not sure how that relates to making love. And I'm not sure if that captures what a painter does, either.

When you talked about surging past, I thought of horse racing. Seeing a horse with a bit to spare coming through to win in the last few yards gives an unbelievable sense of excitement. But there is another ingredient, which comes over in art too, namely courage. When you see two horses battling it out, or two boxers: the tremendous aesthetic excitement that we get from courage! And this sense of courage gives us this powerful aesthetic reaction, yes?

I think so.

Yes, I think we do get this sense of courage in art, in Beethoven, who, again . . . but there it comes back to risk.

And uncompromisingness.

And uncompromisingness.

Think of Rembrandt's self-portraits – a clichéd example, no doubt. You get the feeling that here's a man who's painting himself without any illusions. He's facing the facts. I like the phrase, from the Yorkshire and England batsman Maurice Leyland, who had a rugged and busy style: 'Fast bowling keeps you honest.' Isn't that what we're talking about, a sort of integrity in facing whatever is thrown at you, whatever is an obstacle to your performance from within or without, and seeing it through? I think this gives enormous satisfaction. It's heart-warming. Which means, I suppose, that aesthetic pleasure can't be separated off from moral qualities and human qualities. Uncompromisingness, facing the facts, not turning one's face away, not giving up . . .

All qualities that are used in praise of the arts.

Yes, I agree. I agree.

Exactly analogous.

In fact they're used in respect of every human activity. I mean, a doctor, let's say, or a mother, or someone faced with illness, or deprivation, and the way they courageously find the ways and means to survive it, stick it out and make something of it. And by the same token, cowardice is betrayed as well, failings, weaknesses, tension, over-eagerness to please. It's not restricted to art and sport. But this kind of dishonesty, cheating, honesty, courage comes through in sport and art.

And this is what moves us in sport and art, that it is a paradigm of good qualities.

Sport and art have something else in common. They are set aside from the absolute necessities, the bare necessities of life. And they have a frame round them. The painting with its frame, or the cricket ground with its boundary, or the boxing ring, or whatever. They are framed and set off from ordinary life. This wouldn't be true of everything, of architecture for instance, but it's true of many forms of art and sport. And yet within that frame, there's a possibility of finding many of the qualities in life that we admire or lack in concentrated form. What fascinates us is a moral dimension in a broad sense of 'moral', the dimension of the revelation of human qualities.

Another quality that is revealed is freedom. How free am I? How much am I constrained by anxiety or by fear of failure? Or – here it's back to risk – how free can I be in my mind, with my fantasies? There's a difference here between sport and life, in that sportsmen tend to be conservative, whereas artists tend to be radical. In your book, *About Modern Art* you quote Matisse saying to an American lady journalist: 'Oh, do tell the American people that I am a normal family man; that I am a devoted husband and father, that I have three fine children, that I go to the theatre, ride, have a comfortable home, a fine garden, and that I love flowers, etc., just like any man.' He says this to correct a cliché about artists. A sportsman wouldn't have to tell that story. He might have to tell the public the opposite story: 'Look, I actually enjoy doing something completely outrageous, I can enjoy a work of avant-garde music, and am not a complete freak as a result, or maybe I am, but I don't care.'

A bit earlier you were going to say something and stood back to let me say something that I wanted to say, to do with surging past another horse. Can you remember?

I don't remember – except that what I now think of saying is that if someone merely scuttles past in the last lap, one admires their courage, but if someone lengthens his stride, and cruises past, one has different feelings. It's the same business we've been talking about, of outcome mixed with aesthetic pleasure. That comes back to economy of movement, to the classical, and to that aspect of beauty. We haven't used the word beauty much yet, have we? By the way, Wittgenstein in his conversation on aesthetics says that we use the word 'beauty' rarely; the notion plays little part in our appreciation of pictures or music or whatever. But beauty, nevertheless, is partly to do with making something look simple that isn't. Artists may make efforts to make what they do look easy.

You introduced beauty, but in passing you mentioned something that is absolutely vital that we have not yet mentioned, though it was suggested by various things we've said: that nothing moves us more in the arts than economy of means. One example of which is when a string quartet can be given the richness of a whole orchestra. We get a sense of the person making more of the means he has, and this is one of the main preoccupations of the artist, who will pride himself on using the greatest economy of means. Now to what extent are we right, then, if we say that timing is of the essence, or is it one of several things? Is not the essence, perhaps, economy of means?

No, I think it's one of several things. It's like a cake, you know, there are many essential ingredients. I think there are other elements than both these. Colin Cowdrey, the Kent and England cricketer who was noted for the graceful simplicity of his style, could move the bat a short distance and the ball would speed off – economy of means plus timing – he would just caress the ball. This gave satisfaction. Ian Botham, the fine England all-rounder, and a great hitter, simply heaved, and the ball went miles. There's something admirable and pleasing in both.

Yes.

They're very different things. Then again, the Trinidadian Brian Lara, a wonderful but variable left-handed batsman, offers another element of pleasure; he plays with a little extra flourish, his bat twirls, he picks it up an extra few inches. His bat moves extraordinarily fast in playing a stroke. All three of these things are satisfying in different ways. They all have a shared basic structure; I mean, the bat comes down basically through the line of the ball, and they all hit the ball at more or less the same point in the pendulum swing. All are aesthetically pleasing. But the actual styles are different. Economy of means is one, but only one, of the many factors that appeal to us. I think it satisfies us because of its links with learning. Think of a baby learning to walk. At first it's impossible, incredibly difficult. The baby totters, falls, is caught by father. Gradually he or she can just do it. The same is true of skiing or batting. We gradually learn. So the capacity to perform naturally, with ease, without extraneous fuss, appeals at a deep level to us all.

And the baby's satisfaction?

Yes, enormous satisfaction. I mean, I think doing something with one's body that is difficult, but making it look easy, natural, must be firmly rooted in sport and the pleasures of sport. May I say something else?

Of course.

I was thinking about the layers of meaning in sport and art. I think with art one expects the artist to deal with, portray, the central things in life. I don't know how far that can be taken with sport. But there are Oedipal and sexual analogies to what we do in sport, which link with what you said before about intimacy and timing. For example, isn't there a sexual analogy – meaning, even – in piercing the field, when you push something into a small space or target, as when you score a goal in football? I'm impressed by the remark of Adrian Stokes – who was a psychoanalytically oriented critic and a theorist of art – about batting as a matter of guarding one's 'castle' (jargon for wicket) like an Oedipal father against the sons who assault it and try to knock it over. He's protecting his wife as well as his home. I think that's probably right, and of course there are a lot of rivalrous Oedipal elements which are upfront in sport. Two people (often, but not always, men) fighting each other in one form or another.

Stokes also writes of the more idyllic, pre-Oedipal, aspects of cricket. What takes place has a slow rhythm to it, extending over a long period of time. There are colours, green and white, the sun on the grass, originally a rural setting. Or take another aspect. Cricket consists of a series of somewhat disconnected mini-dramas. Each ball involves two protagonists pitted against each other. But one can see this in a more holistic way; as the bowler runs in, the fielders move in alertly towards the batsman. Then they relax, and drift back. There is an ebb and flow, like breathing, like waves breaking on the beach and then drawing back. The rhythm is of coming together intensely, and moving apart. I think that sort of rhythm echoes deep rhythms in life, including sexual ones. And it's part of the attraction, of the aesthetic.

It's also part of the attraction of horse racing. The horses cantering to the start.

Walking around in the ring.

And walking around in the ring. And all those different rhythms relate to one another, and the pace changes. This offers an artful aesthetic experience, which relates, of course, to changes of pace in music.

Absolutely. And indeed to silence in music.

Indeed.

I was talking earlier about sport as contest, and then of sport as beyond or other than simply contest. This ingress of fielders on the batsman can be seen as a form of hunting; a paranoid experience. One is hemmed in by these hostile fielders, Australians, in green baggy caps, perhaps, with Dennis Lillee, one of the greatest fast bowlers of all time, racing in to bowl, and the crowd baying. But one can see it too as a loving activity, moving close and drawing back, picking up a baby and putting it down, coming together and moving apart. Another thought: when we catch a ball at cricket, we sometimes have the conviction that we are certain to catch it before we do. And there is something containing, holding, being a safe pair of hands, being held by one's parents, in this sort of experience. I wonder how much these thoughts apply also to art.

Absolutely. In art, things come to a rest.

I want to make one more comment about intimacy and pairing in cricket. Most commonly, the bowler is experienced by the batsman simply as his enemy. Occasionally, if I was really feeling okay in myself as a batsman, I had an experience of the bowler as necessary for me, and me for him. I could realise in a full way, on the pulses, that we are both involved in a *joint* activity. He needs a good batsman to bring out the best arts of his bowling, and I need him as an excellent bowler to bring out the arts of my batting. At these rare times, I could feel this sort of oneness with my antagonist. Mostly I was too anxious, or pragmatic, for that, or too insecure; but there were these valuable experiences of a sort of union between us.

As it is in chess.

As it is in chess.

GILBERT & GEORGE 1997

Recorded in 1997, and first published as 'I'll Tell You Where There's Irony in Our Work: Nowhere, Nowhere, Nowhere', in *Modern Painters* in 1998.

We are an artist

DAVID SYLVESTER *Your exhibition at the Ville de Paris [1997] is your first full-scale retrospective, but the show you had in Bologna last year was already something of a retrospective, and I wonder whether you learnt anything by seeing it?*

GILBERT Yes, we did learn something. We learnt that we would like to make a much bigger one.

GEORGE We always say that when we see our works together in that way, which is quite rare, we see how similar our development is to the viewer's life, compared with the normal development you see when you see an artist's retrospective: you see his stylistic development; you see how he changes his shapes or his techniques. Whereas the viewer has a life's development: you're fifteen and you're scared; you're sixteen, you have sex; you're seventeen, you go to college; you have a life story. And our story in the pictures is similar to the viewer's. It's not a stylistic development, it's a content development.

Well, it is a stylistic and technical development too.

GEORGE Serving the content. It's not form for form's sake, it's form for meaning.

GILBERT Form to make it more powerful, form to make the pictures speak louder, form to make it in some way more aggressive. We always like the image to absolutely shout out at the viewer as much as we are able to arrange it. That's why we are teaching ourselves different techniques for manipulating the images all the time. That's why we would never have assistants, because they wouldn't know how to manipulate an image. They would make them all the same, but we are able to increase their power.

GEORGE The idea is always to make pictures that will form all of our futures a little bit. We want life to be different as a result of our exhibitions. We want people to be affected by seeing the pictures. We want them to go home and be different.

When you say people, you don't actually mean just the usual art audience?

GILBERT We mean every single person that lives outside there. Every child, every granny, everybody, black, white, Chinese, everybody. Because we don't believe that art is anything else than speaking to the viewer. It's not making aesthetics for an élite.

You're the opposite of avant-garde artists in that sense. Because avant-garde art is tied up with the notion of making esoteric statements.

GEORGE We don't feel we have to make a comment on art, and we don't even believe that we show life or reflect life, which is what a lot of people think we do. They think our art is somehow related to reality. We don't think that. We think our pictures are about future possibility.

GILBERT It is all based on inner feeling. It is looking inside ourself. We never look at the world. We always try to feel the inside of what is inside our self. That's the window for the world. To look inside.

GEORGE People very often say, 'Oh, but you must get your inspiration from somewhere, you must go to young people's clubs or you must travel or something.' And we say we just go out of the door in the morning, it's raining and there's a pool of vomit there, and there are pigeons pecking away at it, there's a matchstick with a little bit of groundsel growing beside it; everything is in there anyway. There is nothing that is not in that immediate scene. And all of those things are also inside a person, and all over the world.

GILBERT And I must say that all our art in the end is based on the desperation of life. It's very difficult to live. It's very difficult to survive.

GEORGE It's the second most difficult thing in the world, isn't it? And if you remove the culture, then it's totally impossible. If you go to a city where there's no gallery, there's no public library, there's no concert hall, no university, you need a bodyguard and there are dead bodies in the street.

Do you want to bring that desperation out or do you think it comes out anyway?

GILBERT Yes, it is unavoidable. I don't know, maybe we are unhappy people. I don't know if everybody else is very happy. I never felt happy. There are some small moments of happiness, but in general it's miserable. If people look at our art from the beginning to the end, it's in some way based on that, that kind of desperation.

You began as a pair of tramps, in Underneath the Arches.

GEORGE Precisely. We like it very much, we like the words of the song.

GILBERT It's very interesting. Did you read in Lynn Barber's interview that she went to Dartington to find out what George was like at school, and found out what George said when he was young and was asked what he wanted to be.

GEORGE I've forgotten it now.

GILBERT He wanted to be a 'super-tramp'.

GEORGE I'd forgotten that . . . Apparently I said that.

GILBERT And I think that's exactly right.

When you started working together, was it a totally instinctive and emotional thing that brought you together or was it that you'd already formulated similar attitudes?

GEORGE Well, we don't believe in similar attitudes in that way. I think it was a combination of love at first sight and of circumstances. We were already working together before we were even conscious of it. It was something that happened to us, we believe, rather than something we decided. We very often think, even when we're making designs for new pictures, it's as though something else has guided our hand to make the design. 'Did we really do that? Who made us do that? Who made us say this?' We do believe in something over ourselves, outside of ourselves, some power. If not, we wouldn't do pictures like that. We wouldn't consciously do *Naked Shit Pictures*. We are dragged into it in some way.

GILBERT We didn't actually know, but it was some kind of friendship that I always said began because George was the only person who accepted my pidgin English.

GEORGE I think we came together because we were both apart from the crowd at St Martin's. We weren't goody-goody students, we weren't angling for a teaching job, because we knew we'd never get one anyway; we weren't angling for an Arts Council grant to get a studio, because we knew we wouldn't get one anyway. We knew we could never become the normal good student and we accepted that and made it a quality rather than a handicap. We didn't want to be the good student. We knew they were naïve, not us.

GILBERT So we helped each other. I think that is still what is there. I think that we are only total when we are together.

GEORGE And also we should remember that we both realised the limitations of that formalistic art at St Martin's. We saw that all of those sculptures the other chaps were doing could not be taken outside the front door of St Martin's, that they would cease to live in that moment, they would become invisible to those thousands and thousands of fantastic people from all over the world who walk up and down Charing Cross Road.

It was rather like a stroke of fate that not only put you together in the same place, but also organised it so that the place was St Martin's, where there was a certain corporate spirit and a certain complacent formalism. I imagine that that was a marvellous aggravation to you both.

GEORGE I'm sure that's true. It set us apart in that way.

GILBERT But it was very exciting. We liked it. In fact we felt on top of the world. We felt we were arrogant artists, who knew exactly where we were going, and we thought that all these formalistic sculptures were total nonsense. And I think that the biggest luck was that we were able to remove ourselves from the art for art's sake.

GEORGE We fell out of love with art and fell in love with the viewer. I think that was the magic moment.

And when did that happen?

GEORGE I think that it really crystallised at the moment of leaving St Martin's, because we were so crazy and so separate at that moment. We went to the Tate Gallery and said that we would like to present a crib, as they didn't have a crib at the Tate at Christmas time. We said we would get some sheep from the RSPCA and a donkey and we would stand there and be like Mary and Joseph. A fantastic living piece, with the straw on the ground and everything; we could arrange a little star of Bethlehem. They wouldn't do it, but it was an amazing idea. Still would be amazing, don't you think?

GILBERT Because we realised that the world was waiting for some kind of art. We were not too conscious that we were doing it, but then we had this idea out of the blue that we were it. We became some kind of object. Like we went to St Martin's holding our sculptures like a ball and a stick, and that's it. Like George was holding a stick and I was holding a ball. Two people make a composition. One person doesn't.

GEORGE One person looks like a bloody silly artist. We always said that two persons removed self-doubt. We can never have self-doubt. Because the normal artist is always asking himself questions, he is sitting in front of the canvas saying, 'Should I put another green cow in the corner, should I change the colour of the sky?', and no answer comes back. Whereas with two people you've always got an answer. Self-doubt is vanishing. As long as the other one always says yes – and we always say yes to each other. I think we share an enormous sense of purpose. I think that's our greatest strength. We are more concerned with that than with any details.

GILBERT You know, I don't think we are interested in anything else. I have no passionate interests. I have no interest in money, or anything. So in the end it becomes very easy to concentrate totally on this vision.

GEORGE We can be alone together, I think. That's the best thing. Whereas you can't be alone with friends. We don't impose on each other. Therefore we can be alone like a person is alone.

GILBERT I mean we can be alone with some friends, but very few, and if not you always feel people want something from you, and at that moment you are not free.

GEORGE They want something from you all the time. And then you get drunk, you cannot relax. You can only relax with a very few people. Your great good fortune – though it's a very trying thing also and it makes great demands – is working with the person that you're attached to personally. It can be enormously rewarding, and it's also enormously difficult. But it solves a lot of problems if you can manage it, though it also creates problems.

GILBERT We accepted that from the beginning.

GEORGE Our shared sense of purpose is more important than any of the other details of life. The other things don't matter really. If we can make *Shitty Naked Human World*, what the fuck else really matters? We are so proud that we can do a picture like that. Incredibly proud. When we see people standing in front of that picture and chatting amongst themselves, we feel enormously rewarded, because without us they wouldn't have that experience.

Your partnership has lasted much longer than most working partnerships.

GEORGE We never worked together, that's the important difference. We never collaborated. All those partnerships you think of, it's one person doing one thing and another doing another, bringing their different talents to bear on something. We don't think we're doing that. We never see it that we are doing a picture together in that way.

GILBERT That disappeared a long time ago.

GEORGE It disappeared the moment two or three people had said of us, 'Oh, it can never last, because two people can't possibly work out.' We became very determined.

GILBERT We needed each other. We needed each other because we were not total.

GEORGE We don't think we're two artists. We think we are an artist.

To make a frozen moment of feeling

GILBERT We invented a technical form to make our art that doesn't distinguish between us. You don't see the brush strokes, the handwritten message that every artist is so proud of. We always said that we wanted to make pictures that shoot from the brain like a laser beam.

But I must say that at Bologna I loved those early drawings in which you do see the handwritten message.

GEORGE You would.

I already loved them back in the early 1970s, but I always thought of them then as drawings of extraordinary poetic delicacy and charm, but, when I saw them in Bologna, I realised they were more than that. It wasn't just this poetic atmosphere they created; it was also the graphic style – that, as in a Van Gogh drawing, they achieved a transformation of the natural world into a kind of handwriting, they had this quality of transforming everything into signs made with charcoal.

GEORGE Quite coarse, though.

Coarse, yes, but very forceful, and a marvellous total transformation. There was no illustration there, there was a re-creation of what was seen in terms of drawing, in terms of marks on paper. So this makes it all the more curious that you insist that you hated it and wanted to get rid of it. But now I've seen why, because of your remark that only one person can make a drawing, only one person can make a particular mark, and you wanted to get away from that.

GEORGE Yes, and we also wanted to get away from the compliments that we'd had from the viewers – that they loved the technique, they loved the surface, the marks. We had thought we were busy making pictures which were saying something to the viewer, not saying something about charcoal on paper.

Yes, but I think that that is true of a lot of good art, that the art comes unconsciously. I don't think artists make good marks by trying to make good marks. That would be just the way not to.

GEORGE But we didn't like that they didn't say, 'How sad and lonely!' when they looked at the picture. That's what we wanted them to think.

GILBERT When we did the drawings, we had already done photo-works. The first one was in 1969, it was *George the Cunt and Gilbert the Shit*. That was the first of these rude words, calling ourselves names. We loved that piece. I think that was more the real G & G. Then we did the living pieces. Then it became very difficult: you do a living piece and then what do you do? You can't be in every gallery at the same time. We wanted to leave something behind in the galleries, instead of having to be there all the time. So we thought: how could we arrange a G & G atmosphere? So we said, 'Let's do these drawings, let's make drawings that look like we didn't do them, that already existed.' Like drawings that maybe already existed a hundred years before. In a way we wanted to take away the 'artisticness' that looks like a modern drawing. We wanted to make them look like we found them in a box.

GEORGE You know those great documents with a red seal on them that you get in local museums – charter from 1620, with a ribbon in it, with a frayed edge, burnt a bit. We wanted them to look like that. Official.

GILBERT We found them like the Dead Sea Scrolls or something. I mean we found them and that's it.

GEORGE Charters. Documents. Visual letters.

GILBERT Again, we wanted to take away the hand.

The drawings are made up of pages from sketchbooks. Did you both work on the same notebook sheet, or was each individual sheet done by a single person?

GILBERT No, but we put the pages together into the piece that we wanted. We stuck them together with brown paper into a piece like two metres by three metres.

While you were actually working on them?

GILBERT No, first.

GEORGE And we had the negative image in our hand, the hand that didn't have the charcoal. A squared-up image.

GILBERT We did them extremely fast, two to three hours each. Both, over on top of each other we were doing them.

GEORGE Just to finish them. We had no interest in the actual doing of them.

GILBERT But then we didn't like them new, so we stained them with buckets of –

GEORGE – permanganate. Screwed them up even, ironed them out afterwards. As you said, to make them look as though they'd always been there.

And if you'd had the techniques then that you later evolved, those drawings would have been done as photo-pieces?

GEORGE Yes. If we'd then had the technique and the financial resources.

When you started doing the drinking pieces, the first ones were not on a grid.

GEORGE They were in different shapes. Shaped as a person, shaped as a rectangle, shaped as a circle, an oval, shaped as something falling, shaped as a swastika, finally finding our way. It took us many years to end up at a traditional rectangle.

GILBERT But at that time, 1972, '73, I think that drunkenness took over and that's why we did the drinking pieces. We had money for the first time and we did a lot of drinking, a lot of partying.

GEORGE We used drinking as the subject and content. We had artist chums at that time drinking with us and then they would get up the next morning and make these appalling, abstract, cool, sober pictures. We thought that was unfair and unrealistic and dishonest. Why not use drink as the subject? Everyone is drunk, everyone understands drunkenness, even countries that don't have alcohol still have other forms of drunkenness.

GILBERT And I am saying that alcohol took over our lives in some way and made us very desperate. That's why we had titles like *Imprisoned*. We had those. Then we did *Dark Shadow*, the book that you know.

As you said, the drunkenness began because you had the money to drink?

GEORGE Yes. As students we were extremely well-behaved in that sense. We didn't discover bad behaviour at all. We were very grown-up.

I was most drunk when I was seventeen and finished up most evenings lying in the gutter in Soho. I'm ashamed to say that later I lost my taste for extreme drunkenness.

GEORGE You did it very young compared with us.

GILBERT George never lost that. I lost it, because I saw George so drunk, and in that moment I became sober. From that moment I cannot get drunk. When I see George very drunk it's terrifying. I'm terrified of death, of accidents. Two or three or four times he was locked up in prison for being too drunk. Even I ended up in prison. I was the first one.

GEORGE You went to prison first, and I said to you, 'How ridiculous, you don't know how to handle the police. A gentleman would never be taken into a cell and have the door locked. You must have mishandled everything very badly.'

Besides the drunken pictures you also did in the early Seventies a number of photo-pieces such as the Dead Boards *series – a series that has always very much moved me through the way it records the human figure behaving in certain ways in space.*

GEORGE It is more the person being dragged at ever-increasing speed towards the grave, rather than a technical thing to do with space.

You're not trying to convey the sensation of a human figure walking in space, rather like a Giacometti figure?

GILBERT I think that what we have in all the pieces, from the beginning to the end, is this image of people standing still, as still as possible in the world. Frozen. Not too much walking. We want them frozen for ever. In all our images we have that. We have these images of us, people, human beings, who have been frozen. Because only when they are frozen can you look at them. If they start running you cannot look at them. We want to make them more and more still, and more and more that you can actually look at them. You can look inside them. That's why we put paint on our heads when we did *The Singing Sculpture*, so you could actually come near and look at us. And that's what we are doing on the new pieces.

GEORGE We want to be able to freeze thought in a way, to stop the watch, to make a frozen moment of feeling. Because we say if you walk across London Bridge in the morning, you'll probably pass a thousand people, but you won't be able to describe one single person. But if somebody stops you and takes your arm, and says, 'Excuse me, I want to say something to you', you will remember that for years, maybe for ever. It's much easier to remember a picture than reality. We have said to students at St Martin's, 'How many trees are there in the Charing Cross Road?', and everyone said, 'Ah, trick question, there are no trees.' If you go out in the street there are seventeen trees. Seventeen trees in Charing Cross Road and nobody sees them.

What about certain images in the Dead Boards *series in which a single figure is walking, tentatively advancing one leg in front of the other, in the spaces of those rooms with wooden floors and wooden walls?*

GILBERT Those pieces, I remember very well, are based on a living piece – I don't know if you ever saw that piece – *The Red Sculpture*. That is very much based on a very slow-motion walk in the world.

GEORGE The texts from *The Red Boxers* are very much on that subject.

GILBERT We used to send out some of these small cards like *The Red Boxers* and *Wooden Air*. *Wooden* was based on that wooden floor. Again it is always based on this isolation, this loneliness.

GEORGE This is from *The Red Sculpture*. (Reads) 'In the room we looked across the wooden air between. They moved and paused a little, not seeing anything. Leaning on the windowsill a while, two stonish faces on the floor, and tilted, moved on with dry boards and then to stand. Stillness breathing through our air makes us still breathe. Walking across the window glass, dry figures come to them. Back on back, and shooting through the closed study, two in the chapel, with life around the suits.'

Whatever we do, that's it

GILBERT I think there are two different kinds of artist. We always said we only like the artists who actually deal with human life, not the artists who paint a picture which has nothing to do with the artist. I'm not explaining myself very clearly, George.

GEORGE Well, there's the artist who does it for himself and the artist who wants to make a happy life, do good pictures and become respected and have a nice holiday house, nice friends, nice meals. Unlike artists who work by ripping from inside themselves and chucking it on the wall and getting damaged in the process. To run the risk of damaging yourself as an artist is the way to get something so truthful that a lady stops you in the street and nearly sobs when she tells you about some piece you've actually forgotten you ever made. Falling into truth. We'll always remember in Baltimore some woman came up and said *Black Church Face* – the title of one of the pictures – had such an amazing lost look and could have been something to do with a thousand miles away or thirty years ago, but there was an intense connection between her and that picture. A happy artist can't reach that woman.

GILBERT The artist is it, the artist is the canvas. We are becoming it.

GEORGE Living sculptures.

GILBERT We are living sculptures. All the good ones for us are the living monsters, like Van Gogh. He became a living sculpture. Don't you think even Rembrandt became a living sculpture, or Francis Bacon became a living sculpture?

GEORGE The ones who can always speak very clearly from the grave, we think. That's what we'd like to be able to do. If you say William Blake, already I can hear his voice calling, with just the name.

GILBERT That's why we used to like some of the early Samuel Palmer, when he was totally religious and you feel that every picture is based on spunking religion. That's what we like, not the later work when he learnt about art and was finished for ever. That's why we always want not to know.

GEORGE We only want to know one thing, and that's that we're wrong. If you're wrong you have a chance. If you're wrong before you actually step into the studio, you're on the right track.

GILBERT If you know you're wrong, it's fantastic.

GEORGE From our own research we've figured out that nobody created a great work of art, wrote a great novel, because they knew how to do it. It's only people that don't know how to do it that actually do it.

That's the difference between the artist and the entertainer.

GEORGE I think that's probably true as well.

The entertainer knows how to get certain effects, and manipulates those effects; the artist works in order to find out how to do it.

GEORGE So to describe an artist as very polished is the greatest insult obviously.

GILBERT We would like more and more to liberate ourselves from art.

I believe you never edit when you've done a series.

GEORGE We would never think of that, we wouldn't even understand that. How would we know? Sometimes a year later we see more clearly what we've done. We would never select from pictures, or from designs for pictures. Not even provisional designs, not even that. If we design eighteen pictures or twenty-five pictures, those are the ones we will make.

But then when you've done a series, you may not be able to show the entire series. In any case, you yourselves will accept every one of them as valid?

GEORGE Totally, in every single way.

Why?

GEORGE Because if it comes completely blind, out from inside of ourselves, then it must be true. Every picture is true. It would be very cruel and stupid to start destroying pictures.

GILBERT It's just like speaking. You say this, then you say that. Double meanings: it's not based on a straight line. Confusion of thought: we love that. Double meanings, that's what we're all about. We accept everything. We accept the flowers and the shit, the totality of everything. Whatever we do, that's it. Who are we to decide what is good and what is bad, when we are making them completely blind, and we trust our feeling, we trust our inner source, totally?

What do you mean when you say that in making them you're completely blind?

GEORGE We're not conscious, we're never conscious. We have to be completely weird, drugged, zonked, dead-headed. We cannot say, 'What pictures are we going to make today?' What an idiotic idea! What would you do? Trees with monkeys, or . . . I can't think of anything.

GILBERT It's very simple. We always try to look inside ourselves. It's not conscious; we let ourselves be driven. We don't know what we will end up with, we don't know anything. We let ourselves be driven, and that's how we do it, and then we accept it.

GEORGE How would you discriminate between the pictures? It would be impossible at that stage. It would be totally arbitrary. You can't destroy pictures yourself. How would you explain it to the Inland Revenue?

GILBERT But we do make a selection when we make our drawings. We make a selection then, but it is not a very conscious one, because we have so many images – say, ten to twenty thousand images. We always say that we are like chucking a dart in choosing them. It doesn't matter which ones we choose, because the feelings, the messages are already there. The nervous part of our work is taking things, that's the most difficult part.

Taking the photographs?

GEORGE Taking the negatives, the actual negatives.

GILBERT That's the most neurotic part as well, that makes us very neurotic, because once we have that, then it doesn't matter.

And why does it make you neurotic? Because of the intensity of concentration?

GILBERT Even the responsibility. If we're doing the pictures for people, we have to be accurate.

People want a complicated art

Where do you like your work to be seen, ideally?

GILBERT I really like it plastered in museums, plastered on the walls like messages.

GEORGE The profession has yet to realise the enormous hunger for art that is out there. They're perfectly happy if two or three hundred people come in to their museum in a day. If 2 per cent of the population attends a museum show, they are pleased. We think that's nonsense.

You feel that your work speaks to people who don't normally look at art?

GEORGE We feel, from our experience of talking to people on the street or wherever, that people want a complicated art. You see, life is unbelievably difficult for a lot of people: family, drugs, money, education, housing; everyone has amazing disasters in their life –

GILBERT – religiousness, drunkenness –

GEORGE – Muslimism, Christianity, prison, all this stuff makes an enormously complicated life. In every dear little person on the street there's an enormously complicated life going on. It's difficult, and they can only sort out a little bit in their dear heads by reading a novel, seeing some pictures. They need something to relate to, to compare with so as to see how they are. They don't want a simple art.

I am very interested in your comparison to the novel. Is there any other art being made at the moment that is comparable to the novel?

GILBERT Bacon is. He tells a story, or don't you think?

Well, it is interesting that you say that, because he professed to be very much against the telling of a story, but in some of the George Dyer triptychs there is a story, a very strong story.

GILBERT We don't want a story either, but there is a story. We want a certain existence, that is what we want, a certain complex existence.

GEORGE The story is the whole life. All the pictures taken together make a story, not one of the pictures. One day there will be a last G & G picture and then you can read the whole story.

GILBERT We want to create something that is existent, to make something solid, don't you think, George?

GEORGE Something to connect us with the viewer, with the viewer's life.

GILBERT That would be a story. I think what changes people, what you call an art that changes people, is subversive, don't you think? It is underneath, it is not a direct telling you what to think, it is all underneath – subversive, subversive. You ask questions, then the viewer starts to ask questions, and at that moment it works.

I take it that you like to show in museums or public galleries not only because the spaces are larger, but because ordinary people who would not mind going there are put off by the atmosphere of dealers' galleries in fashionable shopping areas.

GEORGE It's more difficult for most people to walk into a West End gallery than to walk into a West End furrier's or a West End jeweller's shop. It's very intimidating.

I find it particularly intimidating in New York, myself. I hardly dare to go into any of them.

GEORGE SoHo is a little different, but Uptown is awkward, yes. Three spotlights on three stupid sculptures and one snotty-nosed girl sitting at the desk looking . . .

GILBERT I can't bear the stuck-up girls and I can't bear the typing.

GEORGE What are they typing, by the way?

GILBERT Because in some ways we like our art to be completely anarchic, down-to-earth, brutal, we don't want it to be made to look exclusive. That's what we are against – lighting them up like holy ghosts.

And also putting a lot of space between them?

GEORGE We are against that because it probably reminds people of a lot of so-called Modern Art which needs that. If you do some damn silly canvas with a black dot in the middle, unless you have it on the wall by itself with two spotlights, nobody would know what the fuck it is. You've got to make it special or it wouldn't be anything anyway. It forces you, like religion makes you wear a hat in church, makes the doors big, heavy doors, has the candles at the end. It forces you to enjoy it. Modern Art had a lot of that in fact, it told everyone they were stupid unless they liked this stuff. We don't think that an artist should use a visual language which eliminates 90 per cent of the population. Because, if you write a book, even on a very complicated, scientific subject, you have to be able to make it explain something. There's no reason why an art work must be completely baffling to anybody.

GILBERT It is really interesting that they all talk about modern artists as if Modern Art were jokes and cynicism.

Can you name an artist today who paints with the kind of earnestness that Bacon did?

GILBERT I think we are that.

But I think that with you one is never sure where there is irony and where there is not.

GEORGE I'll tell you where there's irony in our work: nowhere, nowhere, nowhere. Every time we see that word in an article about us we go to the dictionary and I still don't understand the bloody meaning of the word.

GILBERT And we hate it.

GEORGE If we do a picture called *Urinal*, we can't possibly mean that it must be something else, there must be something behind it, it must be ironic. No. We're doing a picture about urinals and all the different complicated thought around that. No member of the general public ever thinks we are ironic, never. That's a professional idea.

GILBERT I'm convinced that in the moment an art critic takes that away, they will be able to understand us for the first time.

A certain cloud in front of us

When you did The Singing Sculpture *you were there in the work – inevitably, as it was a performance piece. When you went on to do the big drawings and paintings of figures in landscapes, you were still there in the work. This time that wasn't inevitable; it was a choice. Did you have any idea then that, so long as you were working together, you were going to choose to put yourselves in virtually all your images?*

GEORGE It didn't really occur to us that we were doing that. Like when you sign a letter you'll never sign another name; it'll always be your name at the end of the letter. We were just in them like that, as far as we were concerned. We were the art.

GILBERT We do believe that before that we were just experimenting. But then came the moment when we walked out of Fournier Street together and said, 'We are the art.' That was before doing *The Singing Sculpture*. It was shortly after moving to Fournier Street that we decided we were the object and the subject. And I think that was the biggest invention we ever did. After that, that was it. We made a decision, like another artist who tells himself the most important thing is the form. And for us the most important thing was us as objects speaking to the world. And we made a decision, and that's why we started all this telephoning, writing letters, doing drawings. We were talking to the world with small letters, small videos, leaving these drawings behind about us, making us the centre of attention. We made ourselves the object. And after that we realised that it was in some way limited. Maybe we could just make ourselves *The Singing Sculpture*. It was limited by what we could actually say to the world. Except dancing. So we discovered this art form that would put ourselves in the pictures, which was limitless.

Is it like artists obsessively doing self-portraits?

GEORGE We never saw it in terms of self-portraiture really. Not at all. Anyway, for years and years the images we took were of each other, so it wouldn't be a self-portrait anyway.

You always took the pictures of each other?

GEORGE It took us years to work out. They were always separated and put together artificially.

GILBERT In some way we are becoming this object that everybody is allowed to look at. Do you understand, David? We became these objects that you are allowed to look at, everybody's allowed to look. We are opening ourselves up, you are allowed to look. We are making ourselves totally visible in all these complicated ways. That's exactly like going to look at a sculpture, no?

Is it anything to do with the way Picasso constantly put himself into his images? He portrays himself as the artist, as the Minotaur, as the cuckold . . .

GILBERT But he is the painter, he is the painter painting himself, painting a model, he is the painter laughing at the world. But we are it; we are the objects, we are the naked lady. We *are* the naked lady.

Is there a distinction in your works between those where you are the object and those where you are witnesses? There are certain pictures where you appear as the central figures, but there are a lot of other pictures where you appear rather like images of the donors in Renaissance pictures.

GEORGE We don't see it as a distinction so much. Even in the pictures where people say, 'You're not in that picture', we don't see it in that way. We are not pictured as artists anyway. We don't have any equipment. You know, the artist usually stands with a bloody brush and palette! We don't have that. We are there like the viewer is there.

Is it linked, your doing this, to the fact that there are two of you?

GEORGE We couldn't have done *The Singing Sculpture* as a single person.

GILBERT I think that's why we are different to other artists – that we made ourselves the object. I think that is the key point.

GEORGE Every artist always wanted that anyway.

GILBERT Yes, but they never actually did it, they are still in front of the canvas. We are not in front of the canvas, because we are the canvas. So that's it, that's the big difference.

GEORGE And with two, self-doubt is removed immediately.

I know that when I install an exhibition – a process which has some slight resemblance to making art – I prefer to work with somebody else, so that we can bounce ideas off each other – to use a phrase I hate.

GEORGE Not that we do that, but we know what you mean.

But you don't do that?

GILBERT We don't do that.

GEORGE That's what we call a collaboration.

And you don't do that. What do you do?

GILBERT Nothing.

GEORGE That's the weird thing. People say it must be so exciting, two people working together. It must be so stimulating, this exchange. We don't seem to have had this exchange – it doesn't exist.

It's totally telepathic?

GEORGE It's partly telepathic, I'm sure. We just have a common ground of experience, of instinct. If we had to bounce ideas off each other, there'd be battles! Appalling!

GILBERT It is always based on a certain cloud in front of us that we are going towards, a certain cloud. It doesn't have to be written down exactly as it is going to be, but so long as we are going towards it, that's it. At that moment it's all very open, only certain things are very important, the rest is totally unimportant. The most important thing is that our art has to be so human, so based on life, that it is not based on art. We made a big decision a long time ago – that we are it, and it with all our failures and everything. With all our complications, that's what's important. We are not it with only being brilliant, we are it with everything, and that is why it works, because we accept it all in that form which is in front of us.

GEORGE One of our first rules for ourselves was 'Never discuss'. That was in 1970.

TONY CRAGG 2000

This review of the exhibition at Tate Liverpool, *A New Thing Breathing: Recent Work by Tony Cragg*, first appeared in the *London Review of Books*, 27 September 2000.

The debate went on for most of the twentieth century: was its greatest artist Matisse or Picasso? This was perhaps the only century of the millennium in which the championship was a two-horse race – and a very close race, so that there may never be a consensus lasting more than fifty years as to which of them was the winner. Nevertheless, there is a clear distinction in their greatness, one relating purely to its nature, not its degree. It's that Matisse did not possess or need to possess genius.

The definition of genius is implicit in the platitude about its affinity to madness. Reynolds sought to deflate this dramatic notion with down-to-earth talk of an infinite capacity for taking pains. But surely that capacity is more relevant to greatness than specifically to genius; when it accompanies genius, that is probably because genius breeds extreme obsession. Being extreme is one of the attributes of genius. Another is that its operation entails lateral thinking. Another is that it means being a medium rather than a maker: the inventiveness of those who have genius does not seem to come from them but through them.

An artist can be touched with genius without becoming a great artist. And the artist of genius can be a hedgehog or a fox. When a hedgehog of genius alters the course of art, it is through a crucial strategic discovery that changes the rules: the prototype is William Webb Ellis of Rugby School, who playing football one afternoon picked up the ball and ran with it. A fox of genius surprises again and again by the speed and wonder of his inventiveness.

These speculations have come in the wake of seeing an exhibition at the Tate Liverpool of a British sculptor in mid-career who is surely an artist of genius, Tony Cragg. If there's another among that generation in Britain, it must be Gilbert and George, a pair of classic hedgehogs: everything they've done depends from that marvellous wheeze they had as students that a couple of artists could be living sculptures. Cragg is a fox, with a flow of invention that is dazzling and frightening in its prodigality and dottiness.

'A picture, an image or a form,' Cragg once wrote, 'cannot be expressed with a thousand words – not even with a million.' I use this as an excuse for having abandoned an attempt to evoke a number of the shapes, the surfaces, the configurations that occur in his work – if only in the hope of suggesting their sheer diversity. Even in the hands of a much better writer the attempt would be bound to fall short of summoning up the impact of his artefacts: half of their point is the immediacy with which their surprises surge up – surprises such as a set of tables and chairs with vicious little metal hooks dotted across them like chickenpox, surprises that set the nervous system jangling.

A list of the materials he has used does hint at the diversity of the work. Bricks, wooden sticks, rubble, found plastic bottles, found plastic fragments, found painted lengths of wood, wooden boxes, wardrobes, lava, clay, sandstone, rubber, found pieces of metal, wooden boards, plastic piping, glass bottles (clear, coloured or frosted), electric wires, slabs of granite, cast-iron, hardboard, fibreglass, plaster, steel, bronze, aluminium, limestone, lapis lazuli, serpentine, ceramic, a bicycle, marble, sandblasted porcelain, cement, polyester, polystyrene, tufa, wax, volcanic ash and a mosaic of plastic dice used as an epidermis. Cragg's sculptures are responses to these materials. They seem to investigate the materials' natural possibilities in the way that those of chosen musical instruments are investigated by composers such as Berlioz, Stravinsky and Boulez.

The exhibition in Liverpool, Cragg's birthplace, is beautiful in every way: the individual sculptures; the relationships between them created by their placing and the virtual absence of distracting drawings; the rooms themselves, which are those on the building's top floor, only recently opened and by far the best rooms there for their proportions, their design, their daylight and their views of the Mersey. Only one thing about the presentation is jarring. There's a tiny room with a TV and chairs and a good video about Cragg which disrupts the quiet of the adjacent rooms, a quiet that is needed as a background to the imagined sounds of Cragg's sculptures, which can range from a lunar silence to a pastoral murmur to an electrical hum to a mechanical splutter. The disturbance created by the video even when that room is empty suggests that it should have been placed downstairs in the sizeable, uncrowded lobby.

For all the exhibition's beauty, the choice of the works has made it less satisfying and exciting than it could have been. The gallery's director, Lewis

Biggs, begins his catalogue preface with the staggering information that for the last twenty years Cragg has produced 'at least one exhibition every other month, and in many years one exhibition each month', and goes on to regret how few of these have been in Britain. Indeed, the present exhibition, with its thirty-seven sculptures in seven rooms and two giant pieces on a lawn, seems to be the biggest Cragg has ever had here. In the circumstances, I can see no real reason why it is confined to recent work, with half of the sculptures completed in the last fifteen months. I am not for a moment suggesting that it should have been a retrospective: a valid Cragg retrospective, representing his output since 1975, would have to be at least twice the size of this exhibition – and, if the Tate Modern at Bankside knows its business, one will be staged there within the next three or four years. Nevertheless, the present show should have been a bit more retrospective. Public galleries ought to be concerned with displaying the best rather than the newest, and this exhibition would have been greatly strengthened by the presence of a few of the outstanding pieces Cragg has shown in the last two or three years.

I am thinking, for example, of one of the sculptures monstrously spotted with hooks in the 1997 Whitechapel show – the work with several chairs and a piano dating from 1993. And then I'm thinking of the finest piece in glass by Cragg I've ever seen: the orgiastic, cataclysmic version of *Pacific* (1998), that was shown at the Lisson Gallery in 1998–9. I'm also thinking of two of the dice-coated sculptures with a white ground and black spots, the bipartite *Secretions* of 1997 seen at the Whitechapel and the *Secretions* of 1998 at the Lisson. The Liverpool show includes the first piece, dated 2000, to have dice with a black ground and white spots. The effect is intriguingly different: so for those who know the black-on-white pieces, it's frustrating not to see the two sorts side by side, while for those who don't, the white-on-black piece is deprived of some of its meaning. The going-for-newness strategy is a loser in two ways. It lowers the quality of the exhibition and it makes for repetitiveness. Too high a proportion of the pieces are in black bronze, so that an audience unfamiliar with the work as a whole gets no inkling of the diversity of material and consequent diversity of form as well as surface that is one of its prime glories.

In fact, more than half the exhibits are black bronzes, almost all of them members of two series, one of which Cragg calls 'Early Forms', the other 'Envelopes': in the second a bronze shell is perforated by numerous holes through which we usually see a second similar form within. What the 'Early Forms' and the 'Envelopes' have in common, besides being in cast metal, is that their shapes recapitulate the biomorphic abstract vocabulary of typical sculptures of the 1930s by artists such as Henry Moore.

Obviously, one of the qualities most urgently needed in an artist of Cragg's relentless originality is a readiness to be taken for a madman or a fool. Ironically, the biggest risk of that kind Cragg has ever chanced has probably been that of being thought unoriginal in using a language resembling Moore's. Unoriginal and corny. The *point de départ* of Late Modernist sculpture in Britain was Anthony Caro's rejection c.1960 of the great panjandrum whose assistant he had been. Ironically again, some of Caro's early pieces in painted welded steel contained involuntary echoes of Moore's reclining figures. But that is by the way. The polemics of the new movement which took sculpture off the pedestal and placed it on the floor forcefully removed Moore from his pedestal and left him on the floor. So visitors to Cragg's acclaimed show at the Venice Biennale in 1988 were surprised to find themselves admiring sculptures which blatantly looked back to Moore. We were surprised because there had been not the slightest sign of such an interest in his big exhibition at the Hayward only a year before. And it was still more surprising that Cragg of all people could be so corny.

And Cragg has persisted with this biomorphic language: the Liverpool show, indeed, includes several examples in materials other than bronze. One is *Tourist* (2000), in polystyrene and fibreglass: a large baroque undulating ring of ovular shapes which calls to mind the old fairground canopied ride called the Caterpillar; the surface is smooth and white with meandering coloured areas as on a globe. So Cragg has become involved with a range of forms that go back to prehistoric fertility statuettes, forms suggestive of pregnant bellies and the breasts and buttocks that go with them. Moore is not necessarily the main reference for these maternal shapes. Cragg's biomorphs are often more redolent of Hans Arp's, largely because these are less anthropomorphic. Moore's, which are essentially offsprings of Picasso's *Metamorphosis I* and *II* of 1928, are usually variations on a whole human figure or head and shoulders. Cragg's evocations of the human body tend to relate to its parts, external or internal. In any event, the human references have been diminishing. There is no intimation of the human body in *St Gallen* (1997), one of the earlier pieces shown in

Liverpool, with its elegant horizontal spiral movement, while in *Rod* (2000), which follows clearly from it, there is little intimation of organic life of any kind: it evokes machinery – turbines or radiators – as do other recent bronzes such as *Stephenson*, affirming Cragg's perennial attachment to man-made models.

That attachment is at its most explicit in the works that are actual assemblages of found industrial products. These include the group which moves me above all others: those in glass. Some are plain glass, some coloured glass, some sandblasted glass. All sorts of glass containers are incorporated, but the most favoured is a claret bottle – a rewarding shape in that its cylindricality makes it a phallic image while its hollowness makes it an uterine image with a passage leading into and out of it. The containers, which usually seem countless, can be standing up or lying down or placed over spikes issuing in all directions from a tubular metal construction; plate glass is sometimes used horizontally or vertically as a divider. Often a few things are cracked or broken.

There are three glass assemblages at Liverpool, of which the biggest and finest is *Cistern* (1999), in coloured frosted glass and steel. Seen across the room, it doesn't suggest the violent inner movement conveyed by the version of *Pacific* shown at the Lisson. It is only when one closes in that it starts to become animated, with the action growing frantic and furious when one is near enough to feel oneself into the midst of it. All the works in glass accentuate a feeling often induced by Cragg's most typical sculptures – a feeling of danger. The danger is two-edged. There is a threat to the body of the person looking at the thing. And there's a threat contained within the thing itself – a nasty suspicion that it could self-destruct. These fears arise from Cragg's ways of relating the elements of a work so that he seems to be keeping the lid on a potential explosion. And the threats to the spectator and the work alike are heightened in the glass sculptures because of a peculiarity of the material: a glass object can readily get broken and is thus in danger; once it does get broken it gets dangerous. The sense of danger is enhanced when there are already cracks or breaks somewhere. The sculpture becomes a paradigm of reality: death and destruction happen among shimmering reflections of benign light.

I was walking with a stick at the time of my stay in Liverpool. Again and again I had to stop myself from using it on *Cistern* in order to pre-empt a disaster.

RACHEL WHITEREAD 1999

This interview first appeared as 'Carving Space' in *Tate* magazine, Spring 1999.

DAVID SYLVESTER *I'd like to ask you what art by others has especially interested you.*

RACHEL WHITEREAD It might mean talking about my work as well.

The more the better.

When I was a student at Brighton, I was a painter initially, and in the last year of my degree course I realised that I just wasn't interested at all in painting. In the first year I'd been making paintings that were on canvas, and in the second year I'd started making things that came off the wall. In the third year I was casting things and making installations using lines and rubber tubes, bits of old stuff found on the beach. I was very naïve, and at that time I was certainly looking at American art, particularly Eva Hesse and Jackie Windsor and people like that. I then went to the Slade to study sculpture, and I almost didn't want to have too much information from other artists, because I just felt I hadn't found a way through myself. I had teachers such as Antony Gormley and Alison Wilding and Eric Bainbridge, and they were all the young stars who were teaching me at Brighton and then at the Slade. I think they could see things in my work that I couldn't see at that point. Someone like Ed Allington told me to go and see this Louise Bourgeois show years ago at the Serpentine and I was absolutely blown away by it. Then I also started coming to see shows at d'Offay's, and there was a Nauman show at the Whitechapel. I hadn't done much travelling. I had never been to America at that point, so it wasn't as if I was desperately trying to find this way through American art, but I think it was actually the Americans who were influential: people such as Carl Andre and Serra. I was certainly looking at Minimalism and at things that were making art out of nothing, starting with a lump of metal or something. But I was also very interested in Piero della Francesca and Vermeer and painters whose work was absolutely about silence. I suppose that one develops a language, and that's what has continued the development of the work rather than looking at other artists.

You found your own language at an early age.

Well, I remember when I was leaving college and made my show at the Slade. I hid it really. I showed it in the metal workshop and everything was hidden underneath things and behind doors. A lot of people didn't actually see it. I think I didn't really feel ready to show in some ways. And all the work was very autobiographical, and a lot of it was quite sad. So I left the Slade and took on a studio and sat on my own for a year and cried and stared at the wall, or whatever it is I did, totally unable to make anything substantial. There was a woman called Barbara Carlisle, who'd seen my show at the Slade and gave me an exhibition in Islington. She had a small gallery, and I think it was just someone putting faith in me and saying, 'Yes, I think what you're doing's interesting.' It made me focus and I made the very first piece of sculpture that I ever made, really, *Closet*, which was the cast of the inside of a wardrobe covered in black felt. It was based on a sort of childhood experience, and I remember being completely amazed when I actually made this thing and it stood up in the studio and you could walk round it. I've made a sculpture! Finally I've managed to make something that isn't lying on the floor or leaning against a wall or hidden somewhere. It was about making something that was present – present in the world rather than excusing itself.

When you were talking about contemporary influences, you mentioned Nauman, Serra and Andre; but for old art, you named two painters rather than sculptors. If I had been asked to guess what art of the past your work was most related to, I'd have said Egyptian sculpture.

Funnily enough, I'm going to Egypt in two weeks' time. I've always wanted to go there, but have never been. I've spent many hours in the British Museum with Egyptian art. There's a piece I made called *False Doors* that was actually very influenced by Egyptian work in some way. There were these two doors, six blocks of plaster which were very close to the wall, and you would only see the entrance of the doors from the other side of it. It was a very simple piece. It was about false entrances, I suppose – something that looked like absolutely nothing at all, but then you glanced round the side of it and could see this impression. I think there was a kind of Egyptian influence there. But generally not, actually. I recently did a Piero della Francesca tour in Italy and went to the Carrara quarries. What was so extraordinary about this place was the fact that you knew all these people had been there, Michelangelo and people. You could virtually see the evidence on these mountain ranges – the first part of the mountain range was flat where they had just taken off these massive lumps of marble, like with a cheese cutter. Actually that interests me more: the history of where that happened hundreds and hundreds of years ago; how these things went from A to B, massive lumps of stuff, and somehow ended up as the *David*. I was really taken by this notion – I'm not quite sure why. I think the physics or the engineering of how these things were made – also with the Egyptians – is what fascinated me. The Mayans and all sorts of people made these extraordinary structures. It makes building projects like the Millennium Dome now look . . .

Your talking about this makes me perceive a relationship between your work and Stonehenge that, oddly enough, I had not thought about before.

I haven't been there for years but, as a kid, when you were allowed to run around it, I must have been three or four times and was certainly amazed by it.

The sense of the slab with no adornment is relevant.

Also, for instance, with the *Book Corridors* piece. And when I first made *Ghost* I remember someone saying it was like the Egyptian temple that's in the Metropolitan. In this sense it is, but it's not really, it's a room that's been put inside a room. When I made *Ghost*, I was interested in relocating a room, relocating a space from a small domestic house into a big public concrete anonymous place, which is what the museums have done over the world for years and years. It is always a pleasure for me to see this mass of stuff, which has taken months and months to make, finally sitting there with no one around, everything cleared away, walls white, as if it's just blown there. With things like the *Water Tower* project that I have just done in New York, to make something look simple is the hardest thing in the world – to break it down so it's virtually not there. It was a nightmare to make it, and *House* was a nightmare to make – these things that look effortless once they are just sitting there. I think it's about finding the right place for them as well. They have to be sitting in the right place. There's so much public sculpture that doesn't appear effortless; it looks like some mammoth construction has gone on, and it's all about the history of how it has got there rather than looking as if it's just flown there.

It's very interesting that the smaller bookcase piece is in some way close to painting, while the big one has nothing to do with painting at all.

I think my drawings are still very painterly and occasionally I'll make a painterly sculpture. I don't often use colour – it's generally the innate colour of the material. The smaller bookcase piece was almost accidental because I had made these other pieces and realised that the sci-fi and James Bond novels and things with coloured leaves would emboss on the surface of the work. So I decided to make a piece in colour. And just the way the plaster makes the colour bleed is like a watercolour. It's exactly the same process: you apply the plaster with the moisture, and you have to get it at exactly the right time, otherwise it doesn't work. It's really like sitting there doing a watercolour in bright sunlight. It goes all wrong immediately because it's too hot. I haven't said this to anybody before, but there's this very sad, dishevelled old library in Hackney that I go past virtually every day. It has a glass frontage with stands, out of which these old ladies take their books. I hadn't realised until I was making the *Book Corridors* piece that that was where the image had come from. So, there's a lot of real life in my work, I think.

And real death too.

And real death, lots of real death.

Your first bed piece was made very shortly after your father's death?

Yes, the very first piece, the plaster one. It's called *Shallow Breath*.

I'd say that your work is often about redeeming decrepitude, or even redeeming death – the death of places as well as the death of people. Am I being over-romantic?

I think that you're not being over-romantic. That's definitely been in the work and is still in it. But as one develops as an artist, the language becomes the language of the pieces you have made previously, building up a thesaurus, really. A lot of my work is influenced by earlier work, as well as the decrepit libraries of Hackney or the junk shops or the people sleeping in the street, or whatever.

You've had a beautifully organic development so far.

I think a lot of that actually is to do with the fact that, although I've been very pressured in many ways, I have tried to keep it to a minimum. I've been lucky to have had very few gallery shows and a lot of museum exhibitions, so I've had many opportunities to see a lot of work together and realise the path I was going through. There are also things like the Holocaust memorial. When I was asked to put in a proposal, I thought about it very hard, and the reason I agreed was that I had lived in Germany for a year and a half so I felt I wasn't going to a place that I didn't know about. But I went into this thing completely naïvely; not completely naïvely, but I didn't think for a moment that I would win it, I really didn't, and it was more about trying to see if I could make something. I was sort of challenging myself. Then I won it, which was quite a shock, and I've tried to make it happen since then. A lot of my work has been about challenges: challenging how I have made things previously and trying to push things in a way. Again, if you have a lot of commercial pressure, you don't necessarily have the freedom to do that. It depends how people work as artists, but my output is actually quite small and I hope to keep it that way, because I make or am involved with virtually every piece. I'm there from the beginning to the end. I very rarely farm things out and that enables me to keep in touch with it. I think a lot of it is to do with having originally trained as a painter. The surface is absolutely 100 per cent the piece. And if I go to a foundry – I am working in one at the moment – the finish is not really being applied by the artist any more. It's more like putting a patina on something. It is a very traditional process and it looks like a bronze. But I have never been interested in doing that. I remember seeing some Cy Twombly sculptures years ago at the Whitechapel and being really taken with them because I thought they were bronzes that had been painted with white emulsion. I think they are absolutely beautiful, but I don't think they are what I thought they were. I think they are actually patinas. It looked like he had this work that the foundry had spent months and months making and he had just tossed on some white paint at the end of it. So it became something else; it became this almost throwaway gesture on top of this very complicated structure. Maybe it is about having trained as a painter . . .

It would be interesting to see whether you ever resume painting.

Well, a lot of the drawings are like paintings in that they involve colour. I did most of my drawing, I suppose, when I was living in Berlin. Most of them were about getting rid of the drawing: I used Tippex pens the whole time, which is probably a terrible thing to use in terms of stuff falling off the paper at some point. It was all about drawing a line, not being quite right, always using ink and then getting rid of the line with quite a fine white line, building things up in that way and then using a lot of watercolour on top. So they are very painterly drawings.

You were talking about colour in your sculpture and not messing about with the surfaces in the sense of putting on paint to colour them.

A Hundred Spaces, probably the most colourful sculpture I ever made, was a series of one hundred chair spaces, nine different chairs, three different types of resin and three different types of catalyst. By mixing and changing the catalyst I could change the colour without using any pigment. It was a very complicated thing to do. It is about a kind of purity, I suppose, in material. I know the colour's there and I can work with it. With plasters, I looked for dental plasters that were yellow and pink. And a lot of the rubbers I've used have been very like what I imagine the inside of your flesh to look like, very physical in that way. I said to one company I worked with, 'What I want' (I think they thought I was completely mad) 'is that in making this piece' (they were designing a rubber for me) 'don't use any pigment, but just with the materials that you've got I want this to look like the first piss in the morning, I want it to be that colour.' And they were like, 'Oh, okay, we'll try that out.' They made this fantastic colour – never been able to repeat it, but it was a good moment. And the piece was *Mortuary Slab*, in this colour, cast from a mortuary slab.

What do you feel about Brancusi?

Brancoosh.

Brancoosh indeed . . .

What do I feel about him? To be honest, not a great deal. I find him a bit sweet actually.

One might say there was a relationship between your work and stone pieces of his such as The Kiss *and* The Gate of the Kiss.

I was going to say I don't really find them tough enough. I remember years ago seeing a Rückriem show, whom I'm not a great fan of at all, but enjoying the way these things were made and put together, or not made really: just decisions and drillings and breakages and putting back together of the form. I think it's to do with carving, actually. I think it's to do with inventing something, knowing that there was a block there, and then working a form out from within that block. Maybe that's just something to do with the traditions of sculpture and something that I was never interested in. I don't think I've ever carved anything. Maybe I did a bit of woodcarving at one point, but I certainly haven't done any stone-carving.

Tell me more about carving or not carving.

I don't know that there's much more to say, really. If you look at someone like Andre, his early pieces made with wood are incredibly brutal and sort of carved. It seemed to be about making an immediate decision rather than something that you would fiddle around with for hours. It's about a process – of making a mark with a process, or breaking something at a certain point. I suppose the way I make my work, I am sort of carving. If I am making the space under a table, I'm actually carving space, and I decide where the edge of something is going to be and how it's going to be broken up, but it's all done in the negative, knowing that it's going to be filled with the material. I've never really thought about this before, actually. Does that make sense to you? If I'm looking at a mattress and make a decision where it is going to be cut in half, or where the edge of it is going to be, it's really, I suppose, making a decision that you would make if you had a block of something and you were carving it. But I'm doing it backwards.

In the negative?

So maybe I am a carver at heart?

There are basically three kinds of sculpture: carving, modelling and construction or assemblage. I would say your work was really a form of carving.

Yes. That had never ever occurred to me.

The three pieces in your new show which are like tombs, and also the Book Corridors, *are, in concept, carvings, and they have the inner light of stone-carving.*

I had never thought about it before this moment – that it's carving. Especially with the book pieces. I hand-stacked every single stack of books myself and spent quite a long time doing it: if it wasn't quite right, I took them all out and started again.

And physically that is very much assemblage.

Yes, but it's all about knowing exactly what the plaster will do and what colour it will take from the book, what the undulations of the books are going to do. There are some other pieces I have made recently using hard-backed books and then ripping them out. It's an incredibly aggressive thing to do to destroy a lot of books. I always use second-hand ones, but I feel very bad about destroying them, and I always get them pulped afterwards so that they somehow go back into the world, rather than just chucking them in the skip. I have a conscience about it. But with these hard-backed books, you know, you put them in and then they're cast and then you're ripping them out and there is so much of the book actually left in it. Which is why I started to do this, because it leaves a sort of colour of the edge of the jacket and there are bits of paper still attached to it. But it's a really brutal way of making something. All of these things have come out through the frustration of the Holocaust memorial and I think that when that is made I will stop making book pieces. It's a frustration working in the studio miles away from Vienna while all these bureaucrats argue about it. It's my exorcism, being in the studio.

So your work is technically contrary to carving but conceptually a form of carving?

Mmm. This could change my life, this conversation. I'll get all these massive blocks of marble and start.

Well, you spoke with great passion about Carrara.

You know the last thing I want to do is go and order a lump of marble from Carrara. But it was an extraordinary place, absolutely extraordinary. It's white. The air is white and the sky is blue, but everything is white. There's this dust everywhere. And awful, awful sculptures all over the place. Absolutely dreadful. But you go off into the mountains and it's extraordinary. Just these trucks with these massive white lumps, as big as this room, on the back going down these tiny roads. And the way they take the marble out: when it's in the ground, it's very soft, almost like cheese, and they literally use these cables like cutting cheese. Marcus Taylor and I went into these places you weren't supposed to go, where they had signs that said 'No Entry'. We went inside these mountain sides which are like cathedrals of space, where they had taken out these lumps of marble, that go back maybe two hundred, four hundred, five hundred metres, and there were these phenomenal caverns, just completely surrounded by marble. They were just beautiful. It's amazing taking stuff like that out of the earth in that way. There are all these ladders that have been left where you can climb up on to these ledges and walk inside them. It's a bit like in the south of England where they've quarried. Do you know a place called Dancing Ledge in Dorset? They've quarried Portland stone straight into the sea, basically. There are all these beautiful ledges you can walk along, and then they sometimes go to the hillside as well. They are like a man-made Giant's Causeway, but in an organised fashion, so it's all very rigid and angular.

I suddenly thought of scale as you were talking about landscape. Do you have problems deciding the size of the works? Of course, if you are doing a bath, a mattress, or a house, it's given.

Exactly. I don't think I have ever made anything that hasn't been related to my own physicality, my scale. I think that started originally in the studio when I was working on my own and occasionally got trapped underneath one of my sculptures. I remember getting my hand caught underneath something, being stuck there for two hours very late at night, trying to figure out how to release my hand without breaking it or wrecking the sculpture. It's definitely grown out of that very hands-on way of working. The *Water Tower* in New York, despite being the biggest thing other than *House* that I have produced as a single object (most of my works are in sections that stack together), retains that human scale. It is twelve feet high and nine feet wide and it really changes with the light. That was something I wanted when I was making it, but I didn't know if it would work. On a white day you can hardly see it at all, on a blue day it is very blue and like a jewel. At night it's like this smudge, you can just about pick it out. And when it's a full moon it lights the side of it. It's kind of fabulous what it does with light. I was there about three weeks ago and I thought it might have got dirty from the pollution, but it's sparkling. I think it has been raining quite a lot so it just gets cleaned. I was also expecting lots of birds to crap on it, but not a drop.

It was a kind of crazy moment when I was asked to do something over there very soon after *House*. I'd had it with the street and the abuse that I got over *House*. I'd spent a lot of time in New York, but you just can't contend with New York at street level. I didn't want to try to make a sculpture in that chaos. I felt that it needed to be something that you didn't have to look at if you didn't want to. I was there recently and Tony Smith – do you like his work?

I like it very much. I've never been overwhelmed by it as I am by Serra or Judd or Nauman.

There was a piece outside the Seagram building that was fantastic. It was wonderful to see work like that on that scale. There was this fantastic building, then this yellow piece, then these yellow taxis everywhere – exactly the same yellow. Everything worked together. I'm trying to think of great examples of public sculpture; there are so few of them, but the ones that are great are architectural in some way and become part of the city rather than an ornament. You know there is an empty plinth on Trafalgar Square, and I was asked to put in a proposal for it. I thought why on earth do I want to do something in Trafalgar Square? Then I went down there and spent a day looking at it, looking at the buildings and the people, the buses, Nelson's Column, just taking it all in and taking some photographs. It occurred to me that I didn't particularly want to put anything there, but there was something I could do which could work incredibly well – to cast the plinth in a transparent material like that used for the *Water Tower* and invert it so it becomes a mirror of itself: you can see through it and it distorts the buildings. It's almost like making nothing . . . it's a beautiful object, this plinth, and it would become almost like a building and part of the square. I put in this proposal, which was accepted, but at the time I hadn't come across the problems that we encountered when I made the *Water Tower*. It was technically very difficult to make. I'm sure we can overcome the technical problems, but at the moment I'm the only person with the knowledge of how to get this thing going, and what I would like to do is actually say, 'Right, this is what we're going to do; you do it.' Because all the processes involved in the mould-making become so removed from my own hand anyway that I think I could probably get someone else to do it. But the physical problems of the material are phenomenal, and it's whether or not we can do it. We shall see . . . When I realised *House* was going to be on land with grass around it, I thought: fantastic, we'll have this wonderful open space and the ground will become like a plinth, elevating this object. Similarly with the *Water Tower* – the house and the dunnage that it sits on is all part of the architecture of the street. It's not really so different from making something in an interior space. The Holocaust memorial is in quite a small square and the four or five entrances into it are almost like doorways into a room. If someone asked me to make something in a sculpture park, I'd say no. I don't work in that way. It has to be absolutely connected with the street, or connected to our environment. For me, it's not about taking something and putting it there. When I made *House* there was a suggestion that it went to Milton Keynes, which was, for me, a completely barmy idea.

I think you said you didn't want to put it on wheels . . .

I often think about *House*, and I drive past the site regularly. I think if it were still there, it would look so sad, completely covered in graffiti, and I'm sure people would have destroyed it. People became so violent about it, whether they loved it or hated it. They wrote love poems on it; they were absolutely involved with this thing. And then it got all covered in paint. By the end, it looked a bit sad. If we'd been able to care for it, it might have been okay. What makes me really sad is that it never got a chance to become invisible. Every moment that it was up it had to fight for its life. It just didn't have a chance to sit there with any sort of dignity.

On the other hand, here was a piece of thoroughly contemporary art and the public seemed to appreciate it.

And still do, actually. I always think taxi drivers are a very good temperature gauge in society. If I tell them I'm an artist, they'll want to know what kind of stuff I do. Occasionally I say, 'Well, you might have seen something I made years ago called *House*.' They go, 'No, I don't know what you're talking about,' and I say, 'Do you ever drive down Grove Road, in the East End? Do you remember that great big concrete thing?' and they go, 'You made *that*?' and they nearly crash the cab. Then they either say they loved it or hated it. One told me, 'I remember picking someone up from Heathrow, and they said "Take me to the House" and I just drove them all the way.' It was amazing, the sense in the street. When it really kicked in, it was just chaos down there, hundreds and hundreds of people just milling around.

It did have a positive public impact and there may be a lesson there in what does.

I think one of the reasons my work is kind of popular is that it's connected with everybody's lives. People are threatened by modern art. They feel that they can't understand it, that they're not going to be able to understand it, and they immediately put up a barrier. Because so many of my pieces are connected with what everybody has in their homes or relates to in their daily lives, they make them think twice about something. *House* made people think about the places they've lived in, and the walls they live in. Even though it was actually quite a large house, it was incredibly humble. Sort of sobering, I think.

DOUGLAS GORDON 2001

Recorded March 2001 in London. Edited by both participants.

DAVID SYLVESTER *What I'd like to do in this interview is to question you, not about the work you have produced, but about your attitude to an important part of its subject-matter or raw material, namely film, or, to be precise, the commercial cinema. By the way, let me assure you that, if you choose to start talking about your own work, I shan't try and stop you.*

I'd like to begin by asking whether you look at art-house movies in the same way as or differently from Hollywood movies.

DOUGLAS GORDON I think that ways of looking are determined more by the circumstances in which a film is seen, rather than the commercial or alternative intent of the director. When I say circumstances, I try not to be too nostalgic about it, but at the same time, to be quite honest, most of the movies that I have watched, I've watched in bed rather than in a cinema. For me there was no difference between seeing a Truffaut film late at night when I was sixteen in bed watching television, and when I was maybe three, four or five years old, watching a John Ford movie or a Huston movie in bed with my parents. It was not exactly the social context but the physical context of watching that knitted together all of my experience. I've never been conscious of the difference between so-called art-house movies and Hollywood; they were either good films or bad films. The good ones are great and the bad ones you never want to see again. I'm never really conscious of the difference between the *auteur* and the artisan. Maybe I'm trying to be unconscious.

The other day somebody told me about a lecture that they had been to where the lecturer was trying to demonstrate two different categories of movie-making. He took various themes and paired clips which exemplified opposing treatments of them. For example, one of his pairings began with the scene of Bardot dancing in Et Dieu Créa La Femme; *I interrupted my informant saying that the other must have been Karina dancing in* Vivre sa Vie. *And of course it was. So there is a clear difference of attitude between Vadim and Godard, despite the fact that I, like you, would like there not to be.*

Well, I think that probably, in order to enjoy it or even not to enjoy it, one tries to minimalise the difference between the one and the other. One of the problems that I had when I was studying at the Slade School was that I began to lose my enjoyment of cinema, something that had always been a very important part of my life. I like to call it enjoyment because it was time spent not doing something else, the classic idea of escape through cinema, an escape from other things. Towards the end of my two years at school, I ended up in a very strange situation where I was sharing a house in north London with other students from different departments of University College. One of them was a student psychiatrist, Nigel, and when I moved into this house everyone told me to beware of him because he would practise his interview technique on anyone who happened to be around at the time. After a few months of concentrated avoidance, I fell into his trap, of course. Late one night, after a few good beers, we had been discussing music, books, films, and so on, and suddenly he asked me a question. He had noticed that I seemed to have enjoyed a lot of things up until the age of twenty-one or thereabouts. After this time, I had begun to qualify every choice of 'favourite band' or 'favourite film' rather than simply to admit liking the thing. Nigel identified this tendency as beginning at the time when I started my graduate studies in London. And this was, of course, the time when, if you were at art school, you got into structuralist ways to analyse every fucking thing available. And I realised that when I was actually going to the cinema at *that* time, I was thinking more about things which weren't on the screen – maybe the position of the camera, the sound engineer, or whatever extraneous aspect of film-making. Whatever, the bottom line was that I just couldn't *enjoy* it any more. The idea of enjoyment just left me. I needed to get it back, and maybe this is why I'm saying that I tried not to see a difference between the intent of Godard and the intent of Vadim. I tried to compress them in order to enjoy them.

And I know that probably sounds a bit weak, but the theatricality of cinema is to do with enjoyment, to do with using the physical context in order to get out of another one in a way, and the beauty of it for me is that you could sit there and watch absolute shit and think about something else anyway. So for me the whole thing was a conduit through the screen and into something else or somewhere else. It's always been like that for me. And this is maybe where, because art cinema is so dumb sometimes, it makes it easier to see right through what's on the screen and concentrate on what you really wanted to see all along. Sometimes the most boring films are the very best alibi you can find in order to think about an idea that's been burning a hole in your back pocket for ever.

What do you take as an example of dumbness in art cinema?

Godard. Maybe not dumb, but the beautiful blandness of it. But I think especially from a British perspective. I've spent more time laughing at Godard than at Truffaut. Truffaut is comic and funny, beautiful. In a way the seduction of Truffaut for me is too much, it entraps me in the film. The blandness of Godard lets you go through it, it's so dumb in a way.

What were the first so-called art-house films that you recall having seen and recognised as being a different kind of film from Hollywood films? Were they French movies – the nouvelle vague?

Which again I stumbled on by accident when I was maybe fifteen, sixteen years old. I used to work on a late shift in a supermarket, and when I came back home the clock was already at midnight or one a.m., and everyone in the house was already asleep. But I needed to rest and calm down before going to bed. This was around the time in Britain when Channel 4 had just started. It was a very, very important thing – Channel 4 was the only thing on TV at that time of night. They ran a pretty esoteric film series, from what I can remember. And that's how I got to see Godard, that's how I got to see Truffaut, Rohmer and everyone else. As well as the *vague* boys, I also got an introduction to B-movies, or *noirs* – Nicholas Ray or Rudolph Maté or Otto Preminger, for example. And these were the guys who had inspired the early *nouvelle vague* projects too. This was where Godard and all that were coming from. I think the melodrama over the budgetness of it, over the blandness of it, and it's absolutely . . .

But the B-pictures themselves spoke to you?

Yes, much, much more than the films that were in cinemas at that time – things like *Star Wars*, *Jaws* and whatever – great films, of course, but not as influential for me as the movies I'd be watching at home. The cinema was much more of a controlled environment, whereas at home there were always some wisecracks from your Mum or Dad, or someone on the telephone, or ad-libbing the next line or whatever. This happened more with *film noir* and B-movies or westerns than anything else. Our house was much more Sydney Greenstreet, John Wayne and Barbara Stanwyck than Belmondo or Jeanne Moreau.

I said I wasn't going to ask you questions about your work, but I think this one could be allowed. Do you think that you have been using Hollywood films to make works of art? You wouldn't deny that the films you make are works of art?

No.

And do you think that you use them in something of the same spirit in which the nouvelle vague *directors used Hollywood films?*

For different reasons, of course, but definitely, yes, absolutely. It's a shared thing. When I stumbled across this idea that *film noir* had arrived in France after the war and the whole idea of blackness was as much to do with censorship as it was to do with the light effects that were involved – that was more interesting to me because of the whole issue in France; that these films represented something dangerous – as art and as a political vehicle. This represented a shift from the war, an occupied country, and so was a sign for a possible future.

Did you have a preference between gangster films and westerns, or were you interested in both?

Westerns, probably, because I got most of it through television, and westerns were always broadcast in the Sixties and Seventies. Gangster films maybe not so much, I got into that a little later.

In the films that you have made you have clearly chosen subjects that gave you as much as possible to do.

I think that probably when I started I wanted to use movies which were more important for the mythology of the film rather than the film itself: *Psycho* is the obvious one. Once again, this is to do with the way that I grew up with the film. I heard much more about it than I saw of it. The same would apply to Scorcese's *Taxi Driver*. It was talked about in school playgrounds for many years before I ever had a chance to see it. Sometimes the story told after an event can have more impact than being present at the event itself.

And does that apply to Vertigo?

Absolutely. Even although I think *Vertigo* straddles the two kinds of films we have been talking about.

The original is art-house?

Yes. And pop. Both things at the same time.

Is that Hitchcock's closest approach to art-house and pop?

Absolutely.

Is what interests you that it was both art-house and pop?

I think originally it was just the pace of the film, like it doesn't really work in the cinema. It certainly doesn't work on television, and the idea of its not working was more interesting than *Psycho* in a way. The immediacy of that was gratifying very quickly and the constant denial of an ending all the way through *Vertigo* was beautiful. And then at the end you still deny the moment. And that for me made it absolutely not Hollywood cinema, and even beyond the best of the art-house stuff. Constant denial. How can you do that, with James Stewart and Kim Novak? That's just two fingers in the face of everybody; that's what I love about it.

Which version of your film do you prefer? The version where you only see the conductor or the version where you also see the Hitchcock film? Because you've given both as performances.

I spoke to another artist about this and she had seen both versions and she asked me, 'Which is the definitive version?' My reply was that surely I worked fucking hard enough to make this thing live more than one life. Surely it shows that a desire for various edits of work means that there is no need to be definitive.

But you might have made two versions where neither was definitive and you still had a favourite?

I have a favourite, at least for the moment. That will probably change. But for now, I love the version that includes the projection of *Vertigo* in the same space as my *Feature Film*. That's my love, because it's confusing. I loved that when we showed it in London, with a tiny *Vertigo* and a huge *Feature Film*, most people still watched the Hollywood version. Maybe that's perverse, but that's how it is. Even when we went to all this effort to make a film with a great conductor, a huge orchestra, expert sound and film crew, etc. – people will still rather look at Kim Novak and they will still look at James Stewart. They're compelled, in a way.

But the silence enriched the film. The silence vastly enriched the film because it made it more artificial.

The various surfaces I used for projecting the images were very, very important in differentiating a reading of the two images. *Feature Film* was projected onto a large screen, suspended in space; Conlon's image was visible from both sides and physically dominated the entire space. Even when the projector was switched off, the screen itself had a presence that competed with the existing architecture. *Vertigo*, however, was projected onto a nearby wall. The image was much smaller; there was no sound. It felt as though the image could be wiped off, as if, when the projector was switched off, the film had never existed anyway. The original architecture bore no trace of the image that had just been there, seconds before. This made a huge difference in the perception of both images. The difference between a screen and a wall. Beyond the wall was nothing; everyone is aware that it's a wall. But with the screen you always have another side of it, and you know about the projected image from basic childhood experiences at the cinema. You know there's something on the other side of the screen, whether it's a fiction or reality.

So you reverted again to the importance of the physical experience of looking at the film as crucial – back to the experience of sitting up in bed, rather than in the cinema. And again one's awareness of the projection on a wall is different from the projection on a screen. So the physical reality of film is as important to you as it is for a painter, whether working in fresco or whether working in oil on canvas.

Even more than that. I watched a documentary on Picasso recently where they were talking about the different treatment that he would apply, depending on who the sitter was and the relationship with the sitter. For me, it depends who you're lying in bed with, how you receive a film. It's not just that you're outside of cinema. This is an odd thing for my generation where you are aware that films are made for cinema, but you are more likely to watch them at home. If you're lucky you watch them in the bedroom; if you're very, very lucky you're in bed with someone watching. But this other person that you're with and what you're doing with them absolutely affects the way you perceive images and the way you perceive sound. It just seems normal to me to imagine that we've all watched the same film with different people and it absolutely changes the way you read the film. And, maybe more importantly, how you remember the film.

I haven't forgotten that when I first saw Citizen Kane, *one afternoon in 1941, sitting at the back of the stalls in an empty West End cinema, it was already reputed to be a cinematic masterpiece, but I was simultaneously undressing a girl I had just picked up in a bar.*

Next time I see that film I'm going to think of you doing that. That's the social aspect of film; the social aspect of perception of film. I'm interested in it because it's beyond definition, it's beyond a definitive thing. You just told me this story, now this is in here (my head) and I'm going to build this into my next perception of the film. This is a crucial difference between cinema and the other art forms. It's constantly moving and building. Most people don't watch movies on their own, but when you think about going to a museum to look at a painting or a sculpture or whatever, of course there are usually other people there, but you usually don't talk to them and you're certainly not lying in bed with them. It's funny that there's an ironic kind of intimacy around a medium which is commercially vulgar sometimes. It's like the worst possible way to get an idea across, because you have to work with so many other people and compromise so many times, but it's extremely intimate when it comes out the other end. I think with other art forms it's quite the opposite, it's an extremely intimate process: you have a solitary painting or solitary sculpture and then the thing is put into the museum with lots of people milling round. I love that opposite.

When was your first experience of silent pictures? Or maybe it wasn't crucial for you?

But there *are* no silent pictures, because the silence is always filled with something.

What about the piano which accompanied the old silent movies?

The first time I saw a film with a piano player was in Glasgow in 1986/7 and once again it was a Hitchcock film, *The Lodger*, which has become more of an art film than *Vertigo* is *the* art film. And I've only ever seen it on a big screen once, I happened to be with a very special person at the time, and there was also a piano player. There is one scene when the lodger, who is supposed to be Jack the Ripper or whatever, is upstairs and is walking across the floor. The beautiful young daughter of the landlord is downstairs. As far as I can remember, she's also deaf. And even although she cannot possibly hear the footsteps of the lodger, she looks up at the ceiling – which is immediately a beautiful flaw – and the way Hitchcock shot it, it was amazing: a glass floor and ceiling, where you can see the lodger's feet moving across space. It's about deafness and blindness and the fact that the piano player is unnecessary.

There is also a classic kind of western music, which is very strong in The Searchers. *The score in* The Searchers *was very important; would you agree with me?*

Because nothing happens in the movie, something has to take you from one scene to another and the music does this. I always associate *The Searchers* with another film – *Ben-Hur*, because of the desert scenes. The desert obviously is a metaphor for nothingness and no growth and a spiritual wilderness. In *Ben-Hur* the music is much more apparent than in *The Searchers*, where it just becomes part of the landscape; it doesn't exist in a way. I don't even know who wrote the score for *The Searchers*. It just fades in and it takes you across the desert.

Was the fact that nothing much happens in The Searchers *what attracted you to using it?*

I've no idea how many times I saw the film, but I do remember I'd said this in other places at other times, that my confusion about *The Searchers* began when I was a child. It wasn't like a regular western, because nothing much happens. I used to ask my father why there was not more, and he continually told me that the nothingness was what it was all about. And the older I got, the more confused I got; I couldn't understand it. Eventually, I got older and began to come to some kind of understanding of the thing. Maybe now I even think there's too much action.

At the time The Searchers *came out, I never missed a new western and I thought it was (a) the best western I had ever seen and (b) by far the best Ford film I had ever seen. I said to the person I was with: this is Ford's best movie and the* Sight and Sound *reviewers are going to say that it's no good and that* Stagecoach *was twenty times better, and it shows how little they know, because* Stagecoach *is pure kitsch.*

Yes, it's vaudeville, absolutely vaudeville. There's no pace.

Was there more art in The Searchers *than in other Ford films such as* My Darling Clementine, She Wore a Yellow Ribbon, *and so on?*

I know what you're saying, but I don't think it's an art issue. There's not any more art in *Vertigo* than in other movies, but there is a more strong denial of a traditional cinematic 'treat'.

There's more denial of the cinematic treat.

Most people go to the cinema to be entertained, which is different from enjoyment, and I think this is really the critical difference between entertainment and enjoyment.

Tell me what the difference is.

Entertainment gives you an end, and ending, but enjoyment goes on long after. Enjoyment is in your head, but entertainment stops when the curtain closes. Enjoyment can be when you go to sleep and remember things. That probably sounds again a bit nostalgic or something. To me these are the most important times, when you're falling asleep and when you're waking up; your reflection and your memory. This is maybe to do with the way I was brought up; to fall asleep thinking about the day ahead. That's my mother for you. But to go back to *The Searchers*, it's not more arty than other westerns; the most arty western was *High Noon*. Because it's in real time. And it's beautiful for that.

You use the word 'arty'. Was it in the pejorative sense?

No.

You simply mean artistic?

Yes.

Because to me the arty western, in the pejorative sense, is Shane.

For me *Shane* is a beautiful film in a pop sense. I don't think it's arty pejorative at all. It's a beautiful film because it's pop, absolutely pop, because everybody who sees it as a kid . . . it's a children's film . . . it's a film for children. If it was made now it would be made by Disney and it would probably be animated, and the only thing that you or I even would remember from it is what we still remember, which is the kid calling out his name at the end; it would boil down to that.

You've defined the difference between entertainment and enjoyment; what's the difference between entertainment and art?

I hope that art, like enjoyment, doesn't stop. Even the most disturbing art is always enjoyable.

If I may, I'll give you a definition I once arrived at, of the difference between art and entertainment. The entertainer is like the rhetorician: he wants to achieve certain effects which he is aware of wanting to achieve, and his mastery of the medium includes knowing exactly what effects he wants. The artist does not know what he wants to achieve; he goes into the thing with the desire to explore the subject-matter and see what happens. So the artist comes out of creating a work knowing more than he did about the subject, whereas the entertainer has not learnt anything about the subject by doing the work, though he may have learnt something about his craft. And I always considered Hitchcock to be an entertainer.

Absolutely. He knew exactly what he was doing. One can probably be absolutely derogatory towards Godard, but the beauty of Godard is the blandness, putting things out when you've no idea what the reception can be. And that's why he is important.

So you would agree that there is this difference between . . .

Absolutely. You know the film *The Entertainer* with Laurence Olivier, which can illustrate the point quite bluntly. Olivier has one kind of life offstage, where he goes around fucking whoever he wants in an amoral kind of landscape he has made for himself, but when it comes to 'entertaining' he stops misbehaving, goes onstage and does his job, receives applause, and then gets back down to the nasty business of his life when the curtain closes.

Are you interested in stars?

Only in the mythology around them. I don't want to meet them. But they do have a place, and an important one at that. I talked to you about Hitchcock's *Vertigo* and the constant denial of a logical narrative,

constant denial of an ending; these are the sorts of elements that are
supposed to stop people watching films. But the film is carried on the fact
that people want to watch James Stewart, and more than that, Kim
Novak. The viewer need not become a slave of the star by any means. The
star can be used as an alibi for thinking the thoughts that are impossible
to yourself or your companion in a humdrum life. As Kenneth Anger
said, stars are like gods: you need gods in order to think about other
things. That shouldn't be the privilege or the job of artists only.

INDEX

INDEX

INDEX

INDEX